MARGARET
Friend of Orphans

Margaret sits atop her pedestal, one arm around an orphan, symbolic of her life of sacrifice for orphaned children. To the rear, you can see the Louise building and the steeple of St. Theresa's. (Photo by Tracy)

MARGARET
Friend of Orphans

MARY LOU WIDMER

A FIREBIRD PRESS BOOK

PELICAN PUBLISHING COMPANY
Gretna 1998

The word "Pelican" and the depiction of a pelican are trademarks of Pelican Publishing Company, Inc., and are registered in the U.S. Patent and Trademark Office.

Library of Congress Cataloging-in-Publication Data

Widmer, Mary Lou, 1926-
    Margaret, friend of orphans / Mary Lou Widmer.
        p. cm.
    Includes bibliographical references and index.
    ISBN 1-56554-251-7 (hc : alk. paper). — ISBN 1-56554-211-8 (pbk
: alk. paper)
    1. Haughery, Margaret Gaffney. 2. Women philanthropists-
-Louisiana—New Orleans—Biography. 3. Women social reformers-
-Louisiana—New Orleans—Biography. 4. Orphans—Louisiana—
New Orleans—Social conditions. 5. New Orleans, (La.)—History.
I. Title.
HV28. H384W53 1996
362.7'3'092—dc20
    [B]   96-31245
                                                                   CIP

Manufactured in the United States of America

Published by Pelican Publishing Company, Inc.
1101 Monroe Street, Gretna, Louisiana 70053

Since this is a book about a great lady, I'd like to dedicate it to a few great ladies in my life:

To my lovely sisters, Elaine and Terry;
To my sister-in-law, Vernon;
To my lifetime friends, Nellie and Audrey;
And to my friend and business partner, Joan.

You have all touched my life and made it richer.

Contents

Preface

I call this book a docunovel. Every date and place in it has been documented, but I have added dialogue to make it more enjoyable to read.

Something that may cause confusion is the reference to the Sisters of Charity before 1855 and the Daughters of Charity thereafter. In 1855, the order was incorporated as the Daughters of Charity of St. Vincent de Paul of Emmitsburg, Maryland.

A few names had to be created for the story, such as Andrew, Margaret's Negro helper; Mary Lafferty, her cashier; and a few of the orphans. As for the woman who reared Margaret, most sources give the name Mrs. Richards; some say Helen Richards. Some say she was Welsh, some say Episcopalian, some say she and her husband reared Margaret together. All we know for certain is that a Protestant woman named Mrs. Richards cared for her. All other names are accurate, including those of the bishops, priests, nuns, political and military figures, and the orphans' benefactors.

Some sources say she worked in the laundry at the St. Charles Hotel. This is not certain, but because it is possible, I used it. A person as remarkable as Margaret hardly needs to be fictionalized.

Acknowledgments

First I must thank Sheila Larmann, the mover and shaker of all times, who urged me to write this book and brought me lots of research material.

My thanks to Mary Sutton, executive assistant at Associated Catholic Charities and former administrator at St. Elizabeth's Home, for explaining "the evolution of need" over the past 160 years since Margaret came to New Orleans. Thanks to Sister Anthony Barczykowski, D.C., CEO of Associated Catholic Charities, for permission to use pictures and records from St. Elizabeth's and St. Vincent's former orphanages.

Thanks to Sally Schreiber, owner of the former St. Vincent Infant Asylum, now St. Vincent's Guest House, for providing records of 100 years kept by St. Vincent's and pictures of the Sisters with the babies.

Thanks to Sister Mary Hermenia Muldrey, R.S.M., author of *Abounding in Mercy*, for an interview about Margaret Haughery.

Thanks to Mother Christine of the Little Sisters of the Poor for a copy of their *A Little History of the Little Sisters* and the use of a drawing in the booklet.

Thanks to Mr. Waldemar S. Nelson, owner of the former Louise Home, now renovated for apartments, and to his secretary, Miss Nancy Hyver, for providing me with pictures and news articles in the history of the Louise Home, now officially the Louise Day Nursery Building.

Thanks to research librarian Pamela Arcenaux at the Historic New Orleans Collection, to Coralie Davis at the Earl K. Long Library at UNO, to Collin B. Hamer at the New Orleans Public Library, and to Nancy Burris at the Times-Picayune library.

Thanks to Nora Lambert, director of the Rose of Tralee program, who invited me to be a judge in this delightful competition.

Thanks to Rockne L. Moseley, president of the Coliseum Square Association, for reading my last chapter for accuracy.

Thanks to my photographer, Tracy Clouatre, for beautiful photos and excellent reproductions of old photos. Thanks to Raymond Calvert for beautiful ink sketches. And thanks to Father Teodoro Agudo, pastor of St. Theresa of Avila, for lending me treasured old photos for reproduction.

MARGARET
Friend of Orphans

1

Margaret's Tragic Losses

THE BABY GIRL WRAPPED her tiny fingers around Margaret's thumb, and Margaret's eyes filled with tears of joy. Her own beloved little infant. Her little Frances. She and Charles had decided on the name before he left for Ireland. And Margaret thanked God Charles had waited until his baby was born and he had seen her before embarking on his voyage.

Sitting in her rocking chair, Margaret Gaffney Haughery, twenty-two years old, looked around the room she had fixed up for her baby. She had chosen yellow as the predominant color and painted the walls a soft butter shade, with white baseboards and window frames. On the white chest of drawers, Charles had painted tiny, yellow flowers. And from an inexpensive fabric, she had made flowered curtains that hung inside the shuttered windows.

She had asked Charles if he was disappointed that the baby wasn't a boy, and the dear man had said he had always wanted a girl, but Margaret doubted that. All men wanted sons. Well, maybe next time.

Her heart was squeezed by the cold fingers of fear. There might not be a "next time." Charles was a very sick man, in truth, a dying man. He had been sick when they had married the previous year in the Cathedral of the Assumption in Baltimore, and she had known it then. Pallid and weak he was, with that incessant cough. And although he tried to hide it, she had seen him more than once cough so long and so hard that a droplet of blood was visible in his handkerchief. But loving him as she did, how could she say she wouldn't marry him because he was ill?

The doctors in Baltimore had said he had weak lungs. They suggested that Charles and Margaret move to New Orleans, where the climate was warmer and more balmy. They said he might recover in New Orleans. Since they were both immigrants with no family to account to, they moved. But in the months since they had arrived, his health had not improved.

Then a doctor in New Orleans suggested an ocean voyage for his health. Margaret had shrugged inwardly. It was the standard remedy: when all else failed, take an ocean voyage. She couldn't imagine how that would heal failing lungs, but Charles wanted to go. He longed to visit Ireland once more, to see the rolling green hills and the blue lakes of his home.

So, although she was well along in her pregnancy, she had helped him plan for the trip. Charles waited until his baby was born before he left. He had looked more gaunt and pale to Margaret every day.

And now he was gone, they all hoped on his way to recovery. She prayed to the Blessed Virgin Mary for that. She pressed a kiss to the soft, white brow of her sleeping baby. Then getting up, she placed her in the bassinet Charles had made before he left. Margaret had sewn a white organdy skirt for the bassinet and threaded yellow ribbon through its eyelet ruffling. This had been her one concession to extravagance, for Margaret was a very plain person. But for baby Frances, she allowed a little fanciness. What a wonderful thing to have the little warm body to hold in her arms while Charles was gone!

The weeks dragged on until Charles arrived in Ireland. He had his pastor write her pastor at once, as was the custom, and ask that the letter be forwarded to her. Father

Mullon read her the letter, for Margaret could not read.

Charles wrote nothing of his illness, only that the voyage had been long and tiring. But Margaret felt it in her heart. He was getting worse, and now, when he needed her most, they were on opposite sides of the ocean.

She was sorry she had let him go. She loved Charles Haughery, the gentle, kind-hearted immigrant she had met in Baltimore, the man who had courted her and taken her for his bride. But she feared for his life and regretted their separation.

At last the telegram came. Father Mullon knocked at her door, and when she saw his pained expression and the paper in his hand, he didn't have to tell her Charles had died. It had occurred not long after he had arrived in Ireland. There had been no way to save him. Charles had died of consumption, for which there was no cure.

After the priest left, Margaret cried copious tears. She was overwhelmed with an all-consuming grief. Clutching the letter to her breast, she went tearfully to her baby's room and looked at the infant's pink cheeks. She placed her fingers in front of Frances's little mouth to be sure she was breathing. But Margaret cried herself to sleep that night, and many nights thereafter, while she prayed that God would give her the courage to bear this heartache.

Several weeks later, she walked to Frances's bassinet in the early hours of the morning. Frances had not cried to be fed as she usually did around 2 A.M. Margaret knew an unnatural fear as she approached the little bassinet. With trepidation, she lifted the child in her arms and, at once, let out a keening, anguished cry. The child was cold, lifeless. Margaret put the baby on her bed and tried to massage her little wrists. She pressed her lips to the baby's mouth and blew in her own warm breath. But the infant did not stir. Death had taken her in her sleep, and she was gone now, cold and white, her lips blue.

Margaret took the child in her arms and wept until there

were no tears left in her body. She sat in her rocking chair and rocked faster and faster while she held the dead infant in her arms. She weeped and keened and sang lullabies like a mad woman. This could not be happening to her. She couldn't be losing her baby, too. She couldn't be left all alone, *again.* The years stretched before her like a vast desert, where there was no life, no joy, nothing to look forward to—only loneliness and grief.

At last, emptied of strength, she put the baby on her bed. She dressed herself in a calico dress, put on her Quaker bonnet and her shawl, and wrapped her baby in a soft cotton blanket. She left her house and walked to St. Patrick's Church to tell Father Mullon that Frances had died. She needed his help with funeral arrangements.

2

Her Past As an Orphan

MARGARET PLACED THE FLOWERS she'd picked from her garden in front of the tiny white marker of Frances's grave. At least she had a burial place for her baby that she could visit. Her husband's grave was an ocean away.

Margaret found it hard to look at the marker. It told in months how briefly little Frances had been with her. She had made up her mind not to cry any more. She had to get on with her life.

Father Mullon had come with her to the cemetery. He knelt beside her and led her in a brief prayer to the Virgin Mary. Then, with his hand beneath her elbow, he helped her to her feet. They walked a few steps and then sat on a white wrought-iron bench in the shade of an oak tree.

"So, what are you going to do with yourself now," Margaret?" the priest asked.

"I don't know," Margaret said wearily. "Get a job, I s'pose. What little money Charles left me is gone."

"I read an advertisement for a laundress at the St. Charles Hotel in the morning paper. Would you consider that?"

Margaret shrugged. "Sure, I guess so. Why not? I've got t' do somethin'. I have no skills a-tall. I can't read nor write."

"You may have skills you haven't even dreamed of."

Margaret looked at the handsome priest in surprise. "Why would you think that?"

"I don't know. You're quick-witted and bright-eyed and a

19

good talker. You don't know *what* you're capable of. Just because you've never been taught to read and write doesn't mean you *can't*, and it doesn't mean you aren't intelligent. Maybe you're good at something you haven't tried yet."

"Like what?" she asked.

Father Mullon chuckled. "I like your curiosity and your forthrightness, Margaret. Let me ask *you* a question. What would you *like* to do if you had a choice?"

She gazed into space and sighed. "Hold a babe in me arms." Her eyes filled and she blinked the tears away. "Oh, don't worry, Father. I'm not goin' t' go on feelin' sorry for meself. I'm no stranger to death, you know. Nor to bein' alone in the world."

"Tell me about it."

"Me parents and me baby sister died in a fever epidemic in Baltimore in 1822 when I was only nine. Me father died in September, me mother in October," she said dreamily, gazing into space. "And then me baby sister Kathleen died, and I was all alone."

She looked into the priest's kindly, dark eyes. He waited, knowing she would say more. "Me parents had brought their three youngest children with them to America when I was five. They left me three older sisters and brothers in Ireland with an uncle. They planned to send for them when they'd saved the passage money. Me father worked four years, savin' every penny he could t' bring 'em over." She shook her head. "But he never lived t' do that. Those sisters and brothers are grown up and married now, I guess, and probably wouldn't want t' come here even if I knew where t' find 'em."

"Did you ever try to get in touch with them?"

She shook her head. "I can't write, Father. Remember?" She smiled wanly.

"I'd write a letter for you."

"Sure an' I'd thank you. But I can't think about it now."

"Why did your father want to come to America?"

She shrugged. Then suddenly, the corners of her lips turned up in a smile. "Me father alweez said he was an 'uncompromisin' foe of Saxon rule.'" She said this in a deep, stern voice, imitating him, and she raised a finger to make her point.

Father Mullon laughed softly. Margaret was brighter than she knew. "And your mother? Do you remember anything about her?"

"Sure an' I do. Me mother was refined and aristocratic. Soft-spoken. She loved t' tell how she was an O'Rourke, of the royal house of O'Rourkes in Breffni. She was descended, she said, from the O'Rourkes who held the title of Sovereign Prince of Breffni."

The priest smiled. He stroked his square, clean-shaven chin. *Those must have been her mother's exact words,* he thought, *and she's remembered them since she was nine. Quite remarkable!*

"Where are you from, in Ireland? I'm an immigrant myself. I may know the town."

"I was born in Carrigallen, County Leitrim. Do you know the place, Father?"

"Sure an' I do. It wasn't far from me own town," he said.

Margaret gazed back toward the little headstone. "Me parents alweez said their voyage to America took six months," she continued. Then she looked at the priest. "That seems a bit too long to me, but Da said we were storm-tossed and we went off course, and instead of landin' in Boston, like we planned, we arrived in Chesapeake Bay and later settled in Baltimore."

"I see."

"It was in Baltimore that the fever epidemic took me ma and da and little Kathleen."

"And what happened to the third child?"

"I don't know, Father. It was me brother, a year older than me. Sure an' it sounds unlikely t' lose a brother, but when thousands are dyin', people get misplaced. Me parents and me sister were buried so fast, me father's death certificate doesn't even show his first name. They were diggin' huge graves an' pilin' the bodies high for burial." She looked into the priest's eyes. "I remember it well." She gazed out into space and her eyes narrowed. "Then I found meself in the office of a parish priest in Baltimore, and when I asked about me brother, no one knew what had happened to him." She laced her fingers and twisted them in her lap. "I guess he died, too."

"Or maybe he was taken into an orphanage in Baltimore."

Margaret's eyes filled, and she brushed a tear from her cheek. She'd lost her brother. How could anyone lose a brother? She felt ashamed of that.

"So you were alone, then."

"Yes. Alone, an' that's a fact."

"Who took care of *you*?"

"There was a kind lady named Helen Richards who took me in. We met her on the boat comin' over. She was Protestant, but she allowed me t' follow me Catholic religion."

"That was generous of her. But she never taught you to read or write?"

"No. I guess she thought it wasn't important for a girl. Or maybe there were no public schools, or the private schools were too expensive. I never knew why."

"When did you leave her?"

"When I married Charles in 1835. 'Twas only eighteen months ago, but it seems so very long."

"I see. So now you're alone again."

"Yes. But I'll be fine, Father." She sucked in a sob. "Sure an' I will. Soon as I start workin'." She raised her chin and squared her shoulders. "You know, I said what I wanted most was t' hold a babe in me arms." She looked up into the priest's dark eyes. "But it doesn't have to be me *own* babe. I could hold someone else's. I could be a nanny, I think. Or work in a home for the poor little orphans."

"That sounds like a grand idea. Are you sure it wouldn't make you sad?"

"Oh, no," she said quickly. "I could give love to children who've lost their parents. Sure an' I know what it's like to be an orphan. I'd be comfortin' them, and they'd be comfortin' me."

"Sounds most commendable, and very practical. But why not take first things first. Get a job. Take care of your financial obligations. Then one night soon, I'll take you to visit the orphanage of the Sisters of Charity, and we'll see if you can do volunteer work for them."

Margaret brightened visibly. "Will you do that, Father?"

"Of course."

"Where is their orphanage?"

"For now, it's in the Poydras Asylum, but not for long."

"Why not?"

"Well, Julien Poydras died in 1824, you see. He was a wealthy man who'd given his home on Poydras Street to be an orphanage back in 1816. But when he died, the running of the asylum was turned over to a board of lady managers. They taught the children many subjects including religious principles. So, when the Sisters of Charity arrived here in 1830, they were asked to fulfill that obligation of teaching religion. And they agreed. Sister Regis came last spring. She's been in charge since then.

"But now the lady managers are insisting that Presbyterian teachers be associated with the nuns in their daily life and work. And Catholic nuns can't work in a Presbyterian institution. So, the Vicar General of the diocese has told the lady managers that the nuns will be movin' into a home of their own, as soon as they can find one. And of course, money is always the problem."

"I see. Well, I'll go this very day to see about the laundress job. Then I'll take you up on your promise about visitin' the orphan home."

Father Mullon smiled and shook his head. "I'll be waiting to hear from you, Margaret."

Young Margaret meets the children at the Poydras orphanage on her first visit in 1836.

3

A Visit to the Poydras Asylum (1836)

MARGARET DIDN'T MIND DOING LAUNDRY. She had done it all her life. In the home where she grew up, she scrubbed clothes on a washboard and pegged them on a clothesline in the yard. She had done a bit of cooking and housework, too. Her adoptive mother had even taught her to sew, knit, and crochet.

She recalled those days, which were in fact most of her lifetime, as a time of work rather than play. And though she had never thought of it before, she had been little more than a servant in the house. She supposed she owed her foster mother that for taking her in. She was strong and healthy, and the work hadn't been too difficult, but she deeply regretted not being taught to read and write. And not having playmates during her childhood.

Hotel laundry was, however, a lot different from home laundry. Sheets, towels, tablecloths, and napkins made up most of the work. The sheets were large and heavy, and after they had been scrubbed on washboards, they had to be lifted out of the scrub pot with sticks and transferred to boiling-hot rinse pots. It was gruelling work, but she knew she could handle it, and it brought in the money she need-ed for food and rent.

As good as his word, Father Mullon soon came by to tell her he had made arrangements with Sister Regis at the orphanage to bring her there for a visit the following evening. Margaret clasped her hands before her as if in prayer. She was ecstatic.

"Ooh, I wish we could go straight away," she said.

"Tomorrow will come quickly. What time do you get off work?"

"Not until six."

Father Mullon felt a pang of pity. The girl was so young to work so hard and such long hours. But she asked for no sympathy and wanted none. "I'll bring you supper from the rectory," he said. "After you've eaten, we'll go to the orphanage."

The next day, Margaret counted the hours. When the priest arrived, she was too excited to eat. She was eager to be on her way. Father Mullon had a horse and rig tethered outside the tiny shotgun house where Margaret lived.

Margaret thanked her friend for the meal and promised to finish it later. She washed her face, cleaned her teeth, smoothed back her hair to the topknot she wore, and plunked on her bonnet and her shawl. She was ready to go.

The rig clip-clopped along the Belgian-block street, its narrow wooden wheels creaking in the cracks. The ride was not long. Margaret felt as if she could have walked it. Or better yet, she could have run the distance to Poydras Street and gotten there sooner.

The orphanage was not very large, a wooden building in a dilapidated condition at the corner of Julia and St. Charles streets, close by a busy thoroughfare later called Poydras. This was in the Faubourg Sainte Marie, where American enterprise had built a suburb quite different from the old French Quarter.

"Have the sisters been teaching here six years, Father?" Margaret asked.

"That and so much more. At this point, they supervise all the activities of the home."

"And they still must take orders from the lady managers?"

"Well, they don't *own* the home, you see."

Margaret fell silent. It was hard to be a nun; you must do what you are told.

When the rig was braked, she hopped down, not waiting to be helped. Father Mullon shook his head as he smiled. She was still just a girl, for all her troubles. Together they approached the front door, which had once been painted green. The priest dropped the knocker.

In seconds, the door was opened by a smiling nun in a black cap that encased all her hair. Over the cap hung a shoulder-length black veil. She wore a long black dress and around her neck, a silver chain, from which hung a large crucifix.

"Good evenin', Father," she said, smiling brightly. Then she turned to Margaret. "And you must be Margaret Haughery, the young lady Father told us about."

"Yes, Sister," Margaret said, looking impatiently beyond the Sister's shoulder for the children. "I hope we're not disturbin' you."

"Not a-tall. Come in. The children have all had their supper. They now have an hour to play before they wash up for bed. Come along. They're in the dayroom waiting to meet you."

Totally contrary to what she had expected, the children were lined up, waiting in silence to meet their visitor. Little girls, a plethora of them, in every age and size, all giggling, all in need of love and tending. Margaret's heart leapt at the thought of being allowed to do nothing but care for them the rest of her life. If only she didn't have to go to work tomorrow! If only she could curl up here in a corner somewhere, so she could cook for them and dress them and tell them stories!

She turned to Sister Regis, a woman a good deal older than she. The nun locked eyes with Margaret, and that one glance told them both they would be lifetime friends. Their hopes and dreams were the same, to take care of these little girls. Just how this would be accomplished, Margaret had no idea, but she knew deep down in her heart that God had sent her here for a very important reason.

Just then a baby cried, and Margaret's heart lurched. It

was the first time she had heard a baby cry since Frances died. And in the cry of that infant, she heard the voice of God. Another nun, to whom she had not been introduced, moved out of the room and soon returned, holding the crying baby close and rubbing her back gently. The child soon stopped crying and the nun approached Margaret.

Involuntarily, Margaret's arms reached out for the baby. Then self-consciously, she drew them back.

"Would you like to hold her?" the Sister asked.

Margaret's eyes welled. "Yes, if I may." Margaret took the baby in her arms and held her close. Now she could not stop the tears that ran down her cheeks. She rocked the baby from side to side with her body, and the infant was soon asleep again. The Sister took the child and brought her back to her bed.

Margaret turned to Sister Regis. "If I could just work here, cooking for the children and washing them for bed, I would ask nothing more of life."

Sister Regis exchanged glances with Father Mullon. She looked back at Margaret. "We have no money to pay you," she said.

"I wouldn't want any money," Margaret said.

"But how would you get along?" Sister Regis asked. "Out in the world, you must pay rent and buy food, if nothing else."

"Well, I was thinkin' . . ." Margaret looked to Father Mullon for approval. He nodded her on. "If I could live here, in some little space . . . it needn't be large . . . I could give up me house, and I wouldn't have t' pay rent."

Sister Regis smiled. "You'd work for your keep, in other words. For food and shelter?"

"Yes!" Margaret's smile was like a rainbow. "Indeed I would do that. Would it be possible?"

"My dear child," Sister Regis said. "Where have you been? We need you desperately."

Margaret's tears fell freely. "I bring you nothing but myself, and that is yours to do with as you will."

Sister Regis took the young woman in her arms, and both knew they had found a kinship that would endure until death.

"Have you never thought of becoming a nun?" Sister Regis asked.

"No. I was married and I had a child. I lost both me husband and me babe. Me arms are empty." Her voice broke on the words, and she sobbed without shame. "But here," she said, walking into the midst of little girls, maybe forty or fifty of them, who had left their tidy line to come closer and listen to her words, "I could be radiantly happy."

She touched the cheek of a five-year-old, who nestled her face into Margaret's palm. Another little girl, perhaps ten, came close and rested her head against Margaret's ample bosom as Margaret's arms enfolded her.

"You could still be a nun," Sister Regis said, "even though you've been married. You're a widow now, and the Church would accept you."

"No, I must not." Margaret shook her head. "In my heart, I know there is somethin' I must do for these children, somethin' I cannot do if I am inside a convent. I must be free t' go out inter the world."

Sister Regis, following her into the midst of the children, smiled, her own tears brimming. "Then come and live with us. We promise you no fancy food or private bedroom, but I can tell that is not important to you. How soon can you come?"

"Sure an' I'll give up me job tomorra," Margaret said, beaming. "Then I'll pack up me things, and if Father will bring his rig around, I can move in tomorra night."

The children cheered. Margaret's joy was almost more than she could bear. She walked around the room, hugging the children and kissing them. They wanted her. And tomorrow, her life with these little girls would begin.

Margaret and her helper, a familiar sight in the Faubourg Ste. Marie, 1837.

4

Two Cows for the Children: A Legend Begins

"YOU SEE, MARGARET, we need our own home," Sister Regis said as she folded baby diapers. "This home belongs to the Presbyterians now, and it's only through their good graces that we've been allowed to stay this long."

"So what do you plan to do?" Margaret asked, as she helped Sister Regis at the long worktable in the dayroom. The children had been put to bed, and it was their time to talk. Oil lamps gave a soft yellow glow to the room. Margaret was at peace. Whatever problems the nun had, she wanted to share.

Sister shrugged. "I don't know." She sighed. "We need land. We need labor. We need construction materials. Most of all, we need money. And we have so little time. We're only a dozen women and four times that many children. What can *we* do?"

Margaret frowned. "Sister Regis, I think you underestimate the power of women . . . and children. We can beg or borrow. We can ask fer donations. We can appeal to the better nature of men in helpin' our poor little ones. We can flatter 'em inter thinkin' they're our saviors if they put a roof over our heads, and God knows, they *will* be, but they won't know it if we don't tell 'em."

Sister Regis laughed. "Margaret, you're one surprise after another. You're cunning."

"I am that," Margaret said. "I'm Irish, y' know."

"Are ya now?" Sister asked. "Sure an' I nivir would've known it."

They laughed together. Then Margaret became serious. "Now tell me. Have you looked around the neighborhood t' see if there's a house nearby, one already standin', that someone may donate to us?"

"*Donate* to us? Margaret, people don't donate houses."

"They might." She lifted her chin. "Suppose there's an old house that needs repairin', and the owner thinks it would cost too much to bother with it. Maybe he'd move to a better part o' town but he can't sell the house. Maybe he'd be glad just t' have someone livin' in it so it wouldn't be looted or set afire."

"Maybe! Maybe! Margaret," Sister Regis said, shaking her head, "what an imagination you have!"

"Think about it. When you take the children out for walks, keep yer eyes open for an old derelict house. And I'll do the same. And of course it must be big."

"Of course," Sister Regis said, as she rolled her eyes.

"But fer now, fer tomorrow, what d' ya need most?"

"Food for the children. And milk."

"I'll go see Father Mullon. He can arrange a loan for me to buy a cow. No, two cows. At least the children will have milk. And as fer food, I'll take a walk to the French Market, an' St. Mary's Market, too. I'll ask for leftovers, vegetables that're still good, even if they're a coupla days old. Sister Anne and Sister Benedict are wonderful cooks. They can take an old stalk of celery and a bunch of carrots and make a delicious mulligan stew."

"Margaret, you're so young. You think this is all so easy."

"No, not easy." She patted the Sister's hand. "But I think it's possible. An' I have a burnin' need t' try."

"I won't have you makin' a loan in your own name that you can't pay back later and you'll wind up in trouble."

"Sister Regis," Margaret said, becoming serious, "I can't have you sayin', 'Margaret, I won't let you do this fer us and

I won't let you do that fer us.' God sent me here t' work fer you. I'm happy for the first time since me baby died. I have things to accomplish here, and you must give me my head."

The nun looked into Margaret's dark eyes and, for the first time, she understood. This was no fly-by-night idea for Margaret Haughery. It was her destiny. This was their moment of truth. She nodded her consent.

In two days, Father Mullon had arranged for her loan, cosigned it, and cashed the check for her. He knew that Margaret on her own would have been unable to obtain such a loan. But Margaret herself was security enough for him. She would not only pay back the loan, she would make many more loans in her lifetime—larger loans, more important ones, and she would pay them all back. He felt it in his bones. She would become recognized as reliable for her own loans. But that had not happened yet, and he was the one to give her a hand-up for now.

She bought two cows from a dairy in the new American Sector above Canal Street, and she and Sister Regis led them, with their bells clacking, to their new home in the barn behind the orphanage. Each morning, Margaret milked the cows, as the dairyman had shown her, and carried the milk pails indoors. In a few days, she taught Sister Anne how to milk them and relieved herself of that duty.

Two by two, the children were taken by Margaret to visit the cows. They were allowed to pet their foreheads gently, to sit on the milking stool, even to try milking if they asked. The little girls giggled and enjoyed their new pets. They spoke of nothing else at supper. Margaret knew she would have no trouble soliciting help with the milking.

One morning, she approached the vegetable stand at the French Market on the riverfront in the Vieux Carré.

"Good mornin'," she called out gaily to the proprietors. "How're ye keepin?" Many were Irish, having come over to dig the New Basin Canal, which was now nearly finished, and these men had come out of the canal and found other work in the markets. Farming was what they knew best, but New Orleans had no farms. It was a port city where goods were exchanged, but with its large population, the city needed food and manufactured goods, and these were brought in—food from the German Coast upriver and manufactured goods in huge ocean-going vessels from the East Coast and from Europe.

"Keepin' foine," a vendor answered. "Can I help ye?"

Margaret, seeing the red hair and the blue eyes and hearing the Irish burr, spoke a few words in Gaelic that she called up from her childhood. She watched the smile break out on the vendor's face.

"Are you from Ireland, then?" the vendor asked Margaret.

"Yes. From County Leitrim," she said in Gaelic.

"I come from Tipperary. Been here the last five years. And you?"

They spoke for a full ten minutes before Margaret made her business known. Then she reverted to English, since the Gaelic was giving her a headache. The vendor seemed relieved as well.

"I live with the Sisters of Charity and the orphans at the Poydras Asylum," she said. "D' ya know of it?"

"Sure we do. The poor wee bairns. Many of 'em lost thir ma's an' thir da's in the yellow fever a few years back."

"Well, I've come to beg for food for them. Not your good fresh pratties you can sell for a nice price, but yesterday's veggies, or some from the day before. We have wonderful cooks," Margaret said, smiling. "They can make a foine supper for the children with almost anything a-tall." When he hesitated, she added, "I have no money t' give ya, but God will bless ya for your koind heart."

The vendor was in her pocket. "Sure and I'll give you lots to take home to those sweet babies," he said, smiling at his own generosity. "And I'll get me friends to do the same."

Soon he was wandering down the stalls, telling Margaret's story, and pointing to her, at which she would nod to each vendor in turn and smile her most fetching smile. All agreed to send vegetables and flour and meat; and one took a dozen chickens, wings flapping, from their cages, to have their feet tied with twine for the journey home.

"But what will you be carryin' all the food in?" the first vendor asked. "By the way, Miss, me name's Pat," he said, taking off his cap.

"Sure an' I would've bet on it," she answered, laughing heartily now that she had had such success with the vendors. "Mine's Margaret. Now about getting these things home, you'd best let me lay that problem in the lap of Father Mullon. He'll get me transportation."

"Father Mullon, is it?" Pat asked. "The darlin' man. Me very own confessor."

A vendor called from the next stall. "He *needs* his own confessor for all the sins he's got." The other vendors laughed, and Margaret joined in.

"Wait. I'll take you to the Father in me rig," said Pat. "Or better yet, use me rig to take the things home. D' ya have someone to bring it back?"

"I do. I'll let Andrew bring it back. He's our young colored boy. Jack-of-all-trades, Andrew is. An' he can walk home. He's young an' strong."

Within the hour, they were home and the rig had been returned. Margaret knew that from then on she'd have to come with a means of conveyance, for there were generous souls out there who would give what they could for the orphans. She'd hire a dray. She had little money, but she could tell the drayman about the orphans, and the man could do little else but offer the use of it free, and drive it for her in the bargain.

Within an hour after Margaret returned home, the squawking chickens had been guillotined by Sister

Benedict, picked clean of feathers by four of the nuns, relieved of their innards, and washed and cut up for supper.

That night, after a surfeit of chicken and dumplings, and glasses of milk all around, the blissfully full and content children were put to bed. Then over their diaper-folding in the dayroom, Margaret told Sister Regis, "Tomorra, for sure, I'll go lookin' around for a house."

5

"Old Withers": A Temporary Home for the Orphans

EVERY DAY, FOR THE NEXT FEW WEEKS, Margaret set out in the morning with two different children by the hand to look for a house. Sister Regis gave her permission to take children with her on her sorties. It served several purposes. If she came upon a house and had the good fortune to speak to the owner, the presence of orphaned children would certainly push home her point. Secondly, if she went to the market with different children each time, the vendors would more readily believe her stories about the many orphans in the Poydras Asylum.

"Truth t' tell, Sister Regis, I'm doin' me best t' pluck at their heartstrings."

The Sister smiled. "I can't see the harm in that. But surely the vendors would believe your honest eyes."

Margaret tossed her head to one side. "A little insurance never hurt."

Conditions on New Levee Street were deplorable. The road was unpaved and rutted from the wheels of many rigs and wagons. One morning, after a hard rain that had lasted all night, it was a network of muddy rivulets. The water was deeper in the center of the street, for it descended slightly from the curbs to the center, where a shallow canal had been dug for drainage.

Margaret made the children keep to the inside of the wooden sidewalk. She was determined to keep their clothes clean and presentable so as to make a good impression wherever they might beg. Margaret and the children continued on their way, although an unmmistakable stench from the slaughterhouse on the riverfront assailed their nostrils. The children pinched their noses but did not complain. They were on an outing. They were content.

At last, Margaret stopped before a house on New Levee Street, Number 169. It was old and brown and it looked wrinkled, somewhat like the face of the old man standing in its doorway.

A teen-aged colored boy passing by stopped to look at Margaret and the two girls and then at the house. "You ain't thinkin' of goin' in there, is you, Miss?"

Margaret nodded, still watching the man.

"Dat house is haunted, Miss. Dey calls it "Old Withers."

Old Withers. It was an apt name for a house with broken windows and missing shutters. Then, seeing that the man was about to go back inside, she called out.

"Good mornin', sir! How're you keepin' t'day?"

The man turned around, a frown on his face. "Are you addressing me, young lady?" he asked.

"That I am, sir. I was admirin' your house." She and the children walked closer, then they came up the walk.

"*This* house?"

"Yes, sir. Is it your property? Do you live here?"

"Yes, it's mine, and no, I don't live here. For whatever business that is of yours," he said in a curt, disgruntled manner.

"I'm wonderin' if I could come inside and talk t' you? The children are tired. We've walked a long way."

"And what would we have to talk about?"

Did she detect the slightest Irish burr? That always went a long way. "Yer house. I was wonderin' if you'd consider rentin' it to the Sisters of Charity and some well-behaved wee orphan girls who have no home."

"So where do they live now?" he asked, put off by the nerve of the young Irish woman.

"In the Poydras Asylum on Julia Street, but they must leave there soon, and they have no place t' go."

"That's not *my* affair," the man said. "Look, Miss, I don't mean to be rude, but I can't see how I can help you, and I haven't even had my coffee yet. How can you people get up so early and start right inter talkin' business? I don't understand it a-tall."

"No coffee yet! No wonder you're upset!" she said with feigned sympathy. "Would you allow me t' come inside an' fix yer coffee? They tell me I make the best coffee in town." She caught him off guard with an arresting smile.

The man shook his head. His features softened. "All right, come in. But just for a few minutes."

"Sure an' we won't stay long."

Margaret entered the house and found her way to the kitchen. If there was one place she felt at home, it was in a kitchen. With the help of the children, she pumped water, washed the dirty dishes in the dishpan, and straightened the oak dresser. In the process of straightening up she found the canister of coffee and a container of sugar standing in a saucer of water to prevent a parade of ants.

She filled the kettle with water and put a few sticks of wood from the woodbin into the stove. She lit the fire. While the water was boiling, she found a lemon in the food safe. There was no milk for the coffee but if she made it strong and hot, and added sugar and lemon, the *café noir* would suit the crabbiest of men.

Fifteen minutes later, she carried a tray into the living room where the old gentleman was seated in front of the fire. On the tray was a steaming cup of black coffee in a saucer. On a plate were two thick slices of white bread with strawberry jam, all of which she'd found in the food safe in the kitchen. Alongside the dish was a folded white linen napkin and a spoon.

"Here you go, sir," she said, in her most charming manner, "and I hope I didn't keep ya waitin' too long."

Margaret looked him over. He was perhaps fifty years old. He wore a brown crescent moustache and a small beard, both threaded with grey, and he was dressed in a white shirt and dark trousers.

He took one look at the tray and a smile transformed his features. "My dear young woman, where on earth did you come from to fix me such a lovely breakfast this ghastly morning?"

"Ghastly?" Margaret asked. "'Tis a glorious day. It rained last night, but the sun's come through." She walked to his window and drew back his floor-length curtains with tie-backs. Dust puffed out at her touch. The house needed cleaning badly. She looked around. There were cobwebs in the corners. It needed repairs, too, and paint.

"But who *are* you, my dear?" he said, after one taste of the coffee. "And can you come and work for me?"

"Oh, no, sir. I can't do that. I work for the little orphans at the Poydras Asylum."

"Sit down. Sit down," he said, seeing that she was still standing. Margaret sat in a wingback chair facing him, and taking their cue from her, the children sat on the floor. They didn't speak. Margaret wondered if he even noticed them.

"Me name is Margaret," she said, "and these are two of me charges. Evelyn . . . ," she waited while Evelyn stood up, bobbed a curtsey, and sat back down, " . . . and Mary." Mary did the same.

The man nodded at the children. "Margaret what?"

"Haughery. But it's such a hard name. Everyone calls me Margaret, even the children."

"And I am Joseph Kennedy, Judge Kennedy. You said you wanted to talk about my house, though I can't imagine why." He took a bite of his bread and jam.

"First let me put a log on your fire," Margaret said. She did this and waited until the flame from the embers had caught and a lick of fire rose in front and behind it. Then she sat back down in her chair.

"The Poydras Asylum has been turned over to the Presbyterians," she said. "Did you know that?"

"No. Should I?"

"No, I suppose not. Are you a Catholic?"

"I am. Haven't been to Mass lately, but I'm Catholic."

"Then you will understand. The Sisters of Charity, who run the Asylum, cannot work in a Protestant orphanage."

"No, I suppose not." He sipped his coffee.

"So they need a house to live in. And they need it now."

"So?"

"Well, you have this house, and you said you don't live in it, so why not make it up t' God fer not goin' to Mass lately, and let the children use it?"

"Use it?" he fairly shrieked. "You mean, *live* in it?"

"But of course. Why not? Where are *you* livin' now?"

"I'm living uptown with my son in a fine new house."

"Then you don't need *this* one."

The old man snorted a laugh. "Did it ever occur to you that some people own two houses? Some own many more than that."

"But why?"

"For money, of course. They can sell the other houses, or rent them."

"Oh, you'll never sell this house," Margaret said. "Not in the shape it's in. So why not put it to some good use?"

"Do you expect me to make a gift of my house to a bunch of rowdy children?"

"First of all, they are not in the least bit rowdy. Have you ever seen more well behaved little girls than these?" She waved in the direction of Mary and Evelyn, who were silently sitting on the floor with their legs crossed and their hands in their laps.

He looked at them, then back at Margaret.

"And fer sure we wouldn't expect you t' make 'em a gift of your house," Margaret said.

"Well, I'm glad we got that straight."

"Just let them live here, rent-free, and we will get volunteer laborers to repair the place, fix the shutters, replace the broken windows, and paint inside and out. Come back in a month and you'll think you have a new house."

She waited. He put the last piece of bread and jam in his mouth and touched his lips with a napkin. "Did anyone ever tell you that you have a lot of nerve, Miss Margaret?"

"Oh, yes. All the time. But I'm not askin' fer anything for meself, so I suppose that's why I don't hold back." She smiled coyly and waited.

"You don't hold back, that's for sure."

"Besides, it won't be forever. We're goin' t' raise some money t' build a brand-new orphanage of our own, and then you'll have a renovay-ted house that you can sell for twice what it's worth today."

Kennedy smiled and shook his head. "If I had an insurance company, I'd hire you to sell for me."

"A woman?" she asked. "Sellin' insurance?"

"You're one of a kind, Miss Margaret," Kennedy said. "And you can have the house, rent-free, on one condition." He held up a bony finger.

Margaret tried to control her joy. She clasped her hands before her. The children shot to their feet, but uttered not a word. "Yes, sir. Anything," Margaret said.

"When I come to visit, I want you to fix me a cup of coffee and some bread and jam. Just like this." He pointed to his tray.

"I'll fix it better," she said, feeling ready to explode. "I'll have cream for yer coffee and butter for yer bread."

"No. I want it just like this, Miss Margaret."

"Then you shall have it, sir." And she released a girlish giggle she could no longer restrain.

6

New Orleans Female Orphan Asylum (1840)

"YOU WORKED A MIRACLE, MARGARET!" Father Mullon said.

"Pshhh," Margaret said with an upward flick of the wrist to dismiss the compliment. "Nivir you mind! Judge Kennedy was just a grouchy old man whose feathers were ruffled and he hadn't had his mornin' coffee yet," she said, raising her eyebrows.

"But you knew how to smooth those ruffled feathers," the priest said, laughing, "and you must make a very good cup of coffee."

Margaret smiled, pleased at his words. "He has all the world t' gain by lettin' us use the place. We'll make it look like new again."

Father Mullon raised one eyebrow. "And who do you think will do all the labor?"

"Oh, all yer young men from St. Patrick's. I know you must have strappin' young men who'll work for orphans an' the glory of God," she said dramatically.

"Pretty sure of yourself, aren't you?" he asked.

"And when we build our own place," Margaret went on, "the judge can sell 'Old Withers' fer a much better price than he'd ever get now."

Father Mullon smiled at her confidence. *We,* she was saying, as though she were indeed a part of the institution. And of course, she was. He was amazed, as always, at her energy and resourcefulness. For a small woman with the

43

smooth, fair complexion and rosy cheeks of an Irish child, she had a will of iron. She and Sister Regis were the best of friends with the same ideas, and the children all loved "Margaret," whom they called by her given name. They all wondered what they had done before she came along.

"One thing worries me, Father," she said. "When we move into 'Old Withers,' d' ya think we'll be too close t' the river on New Levee Street . . . fer the safety of the children, I mean?"

"Oh, no, Margaret, you won't be. The batture land is quite safe, and you'll be a few blocks away from the river."

Margaret nodded, still wearing a worried frown.

"You see, this side of the river is a building bank." Margaret frowned again, not understanding. "In the last few decades," the priest continued, "the current has been taking land from the west bank and depositing it over here on the east bank. So where you'll be on New Levee Street will keep getting farther and farther away from the river."

"Sure an' I'm glad to hear that," Margaret said.

"The river wants to run straight to the Gulf of Mexico," Father Mullon said, "but in its present course, it twists and turns for hundreds of miles. Have you ever seen it on a map?"

"That I have, Father."

"Well, you know how it winds around. And with its strong current, it keeps on carvin' out soil from one side, puttin' it on the other, and tryin' to jump its banks and make a straight lunge for the Gulf."

"Will it ever do that, Father, d' ya think?"

"It *has* done it several times in the past."

"Sweet Mother Mary!" Margaret exclaimed. "When was the last toime?"

"Oh, about twelve hundred years ago."

"D' you think it's gettin' ready t' do it again?"

"I wouldn't be frettin' over it, Margaret." Father chuckled. "No use worryin' about things you can't do anything about, like hurricanes and crevasses an' such."

Margaret nodded. If Father Mullon was not going to worry, she would not worry either. More pressing problems were at their doorstep.

On October 25, 1836, the Sisters of Charity, Margaret Haughery, and several dozen orphan girls moved into "Old Withers" at 169 New Levee Street. It had been scrubbed and made safe by a work force of young men from St. Patrick's Church under the supervision of Father Mullon. Cobwebs had been broomed down, a coat of paint applied, and flour-sack curtains sewn and hung by the ladies of the parish. The new asylum was to be called St. Patrick's, since it was in St. Patrick's parish.

Margaret had spread the word among her vendor friends at St. Mary's Market and the French Market that the neighbors might donate baby beds their chidlren had outgrown, as well as old cots, and whatever sheets and towels they could spare. The new location would also need chairs and tables and chests for the children's clothes, "few though they be," she added, wistfully. This little phrase always brought another dime or two from a neighbor's purse. And Margaret was not shy when she was begging for God.

Truth to tell, she recalled one washday when she and Sister Regis had wrapped the children in bedsheets while their day clothes were being washed and pegged on a line.

Neighbors, even people from the French Quarter and the scattered neighborhoods upriver, brought furnishings, money, and food to the orphanage on an appointed day. It was an auspicious beginning.

This was the start of an epic of twenty-seven years of sacrifices and heroic devotion to the motherless children of New Orleans by two saintly women, to be followed by almost twenty more years by Margaret alone, for she would outlive Sister Regis and go on buying businesses and giving her profits to orphans and the poor.

Margaret's cows yielded such quantities of milk, over and above what was needed for the children, that with her profits from the sale of the extra milk, she bought two more cows, and later on two more, until at last she established a thriving dairy of forty cows in the uptown section of the city.

The good, rich milk she sold and the cream and butter the teen-age girls made were welcomed at every door. She became a well-known sight in the Irish neighborhood as she pushed her cart with the colored boy named Andrew who had worked for Sister Regis for years.

Her trade was a "blind" for the children. At each stop, she mentioned *inadvertently* how difficult it was these days to obtain enough food to feed so many orphans and how it broke her heart to see the little ones go to bed hungry. At once the housewife would ask her to wait while she packaged leftover food from the previous evening's meal. Those who had no leftovers gave money.

The vendors in St. Mary's Market and the French Market continued with their generosity, and one day, a vendor at the French Market suggested she stop at the rear of a Vieux Carré restaurant nearby, and a hotel in the Quarter, and ask if there were vegetables left over from yesterday's fare, or perhaps bread or a bit of meat. Margaret found this to be the best suggestion ever, and she determined to send a few more helpers to "beg" at other restaurants. She never returned from her route without the evening meal in baskets and containers sitting atop her milk cans.

Margaret and the Sisters spent three years in the house on New Levee Street under the most difficult of circumstances. The Panic of 1837 had dire effects on the economy of the city, and even the vendors had little to give Margaret for the orphans. During those years, the number of orphans grew to 134, and conditions were past being crowded.

At last the *real* miracle happened in 1838. The first Margaret heard of it was when she returned from her milk route one evening. She was coming in at the back door just as Father Mullon was telling Sister Regis good-bye at the front.

"I can't believe we'll have an orphanage of our very own," Sister was saying. "It's truly the work of God."

". . . and of two very generous families," the Father added. "I never forget to give credit to the good people of this world."

"Of course, Father," Sister agreed. And he left so suddenly that Margaret saw only the back of his cassock as he descended the steps two at a time and rushed toward his rig.

"What's happened, Sister?" Margaret asked, a smile starting.

"You won't believe it." Sister could not hold back a happy sob.

"Tell me." Margaret took her hand and led her to a chair. Then she herself sat down, took off her bonnet, and waited, her eyes wide with anticipation.

"Now this is a little bit complicated," Sister Regis began. "There was a Madame Therese Perie Saulet, a widow, who'd made it known when she was alive that she intended to donate a square of land for charitable purposes, but she died without ever having carried out her plan."

"I see." Margaret nodded her on.

"Then, finally—" the Sister stopped to pick up a letter Father Mullon had received from Bishop Blanc and put on her square spectacles. "Let me read it. 'On November 19, 1838, Madame Saulet's daughters, Marie Azelie Saulet Foucher and Marie Heloise Saulet DeGruy, gave authorization to settle with the heirs of Mele Foucher, and all agreed to carry out the wishes of the late Mme. Therese Saulet.'" She let out an audible sigh at the end of the difficult sentence.

"Sister, you say those French names so well, for an Irish lass." Margaret laughed with Sister Regis; they were both delighted at what portended to be a windfall. "So then, what happened?"

"The square was donated by the two families to Bishop Blanc. It is bounded by Clio, Erato, Prytania, and Coliseum."

Margaret put her hands to her face and her mouth made an *O.*

"And," the Sister continued, "the deed stipulates that the recipient 'build all structures necessary to establish a haven or asylum for Catholic orphans . . .'"

Margaret gasped.

Sister Regis continued reading, "'. . . and/or a church, and that the Bishop will not sell any part of the property, and if in ten years the purpose of the donation has not been carried out, the deed will become null and void, and the property will revert to Thomas Saulet.'"

Margaret bit at her bottom lip, not wanting to think of that possibility. "And how do *we* fit into it?" she asked eagerly.

"Before I tell you that, let me read the rest," Sister Regis said. "'It was also stipulated that the church to be built would be called St. Theresa of Avila for the patron saint of Mrs. Therese Saulet, and that the two front pews would be reserved, one for the family of Mrs. Louis Foucher and the other for the family of Mrs. François Saulet.'"

"Yes . . . and," Margaret urged.

"And Bishop Blanc has asked the Sisters of Charity . . ."

Margaret smiled, and Sister joined her, taking her hand gently, "if we would move into the new orphanage when it was built."

"Sister Regis, I'm sure you told him yes."

"Father Mullon told him *for* us, before even asking us, he was so sure of the answer."

Tears welled in Margaret's eyes, and she held the Sister's hands in a firm embrace. The two Irish ladies would have leapt to their feet and danced a jig, had they not been afraid the children would come in and catch them in the act.

"So when will we be movin'?" Margaret asked.

"My dear Margaret, pray for patience. The first brick has not yet been laid."

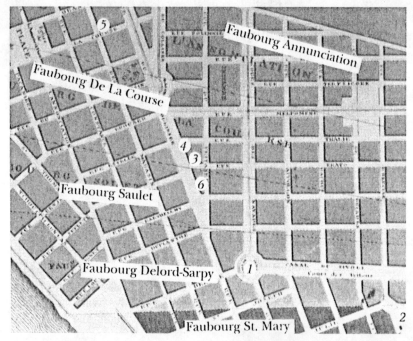

Map showing subdivision of five former plantations into faubourgs. Plan by city surveyor Jacques Tanesse, 1817. (The original map is from the collection of Samuel Wilson, Jr. The English names and important locations in Margaret's life have been added by Mary Lou Widmer.)

1. *Tivoli Circle (Lee Circle)*
2. *Turning Basin, New Orleans Navigation Canal (1838)*
3. *New Orleans Female Orphan Asylum (1840)*
4. *St. Theresa of Avila Church (1848)*
5. *St. Vincent Infant Asylum (1858)*
6. *Margaret's statue (1884)*

7

Background of Faubourg Ste. Marie, 1800-1840

MARGARET AND HER HELPER ANDREW walked their route down Tchoupitoulas Street to the Commons, then back up Magazine Street and down Camp, sometimes taking a rest in the park that was now called Lafayette Square, since the Marquis de Lafayette had visited New Orleans in 1825.

From Father Mullon, she learned that this very land they walked along had been the estate of Beltram Gravier until the end of the previous century, when he decided to partition it into lots. In doing so, he made the first move toward spreading the population of the city beyond the Vieux Carré upriver along the Tchoupitoulas Road.

The new neighborhood had first been called Ville Gravier. Then, after Madame Gravier died, the name was changed to Faubourg Sainte Marie (or as the Americans said, St. Mary) in her memory. This and the Delord-Sarpy plantation had previously been part of the old Jesuit plantation, which had been confiscated in 1763 when the Jesuits were banished from the colony.

Margaret had heard a great deal about two businessmen who gave tremendous impetus to the development of the neighborhood. One was a Canadian of American descent, Samuel J. Peters, and the other, a British actor, James Caldwell. Their building projects, business houses, and Caldwell's gas works and American Theatre had done much for the development of Faubourg Ste. Marie, which was also called the American Sector.

The Louisiana Purchase had brought such an influx of immigrants from the East Coast that now, in the 1830s, lots were selling like hotcakes and houses were going up seemingly overnight.

She heard, too, about a brilliant Free Man of Color, Barthélémy Lafon, an architect and surveyor, who had laid out the plan to subdivide all the plantations between Canal Street and Felicity. Everyone said his plan was ingenious. Margaret hoped to meet Mr. Lafon some day.

In Lafon's design, the streets conformed to the fan-shaped boundaries of the plantations and followed the bend in the river, so that streets paralleling the river roughly followed its curve. Cross streets running away from the river formed a pattern like pleats in an accordion when squeezed at the top. This resulted in some oddly angled intersections, which caused Margaret to become turned around when making her route in the beginning. But it was a good plan because it made possible the use of the high ground along the river.

Margaret had not lived in New Orleans long when she discovered that great hostility existed between the Creoles in the Vieux Carré and the "Americans" in Faubourg Ste. Marie. It finally reached a point where the two could no longer live together in peace and harmony.

By 1836, the year Margaret arrived in New Orleans, the city had split up into three municipalities, each with its own councilmen, its own laws, and its own taxes and improvements. The Vieux Carré was the First Municipality; Faubourg Ste. Marie, the Second; and Faubourg Marigny below Esplanade, the Third. But Margaret covered them all when making her rounds and discovered that charity knew no boundaries and that most people in the city had good and generous hearts.

When Margaret and Andrew walked to the French

Market, they sometimes stopped and sat on a cotton bale on the riverfront to rest and watch the activity. It was all so interesting to Margaret. Since the Louisiana Purchase, the river had become a highway for boats coming south to New Orleans with cotton and manufactured goods. The levee was a beehive of activity with people of all nations and colors, with boxes, barrels, kegs, hogsheads of sugar, and great quantities of pork, flour, lard, and grain. The wharves were lined for miles with ships, steamers, flatboats, and keelboats. New Orleans was a prosperous city enjoying the fruits of its labors in a period of peace.

Many of the flatboatsmen settled in Faubourg Ste. Marie. Warehouses and cotton presses sprang up on streets near the riverbanks. Also coming into this section and into the land upriver were so many Irish immigrants that in time it came to be known as the Irish Channel.

In 1833, just shortly before Margaret arrived in New Orleans, St. Patrick's Church had been built on Camp Street to provide for the spiritual needs of Irish Catholics in Faubourg Ste. Marie. It was a magnificent church, now under the direction of Margaret's friend, Father Ignatius Mullon.

Creole plantation owners farther upriver soon began subdividing their vast estates and selling lots closer and closer to Felicity Street, the boundary between Orleans and Jefferson parishes.

As the batture at the riverfront deepened, several more streets were laid out. Moving inland, the streets were named Tchoupitoulas, Constance, Magazine, Camp, Prytania, Nyades (St. Charles Avenue), Carondelet, Baronne, and Dryades (South Rampart). The cross streets were Gravier, Poydras, Girod, Julia, and Foucher. Margaret memorized them all, for she could not read street signs, but she was doing her best to learn.

The New Orleans and Carrollton Railroad began running in 1835 on Nyades (St. Charles Avenue) and provided transportation into the new faubourg and hastened development. In 1838, as Margaret walked her milk route, the site that would later be St. Theresa's Church and Orphan Asylum was still listed in the city records as a public square. This part of the city was sparsely developed as far back from the river as Claiborne Avenue.

The real stimulus to the economy in the Second Municipality was the digging of the New Basin Canal from Rampart Street to Lake Pontchartrain, which was accomplished mostly by Irish immigrants in the middle 1830s. On the streets near the river, warehouses, cotton presses, distilleries, and stores proliferated in anticipation of the canal's completion. And into this area came not only Irishmen but also Creole families, French families, and a good number of German families, all of them buying homes and settling down.

The first Margaret learned of the Sisters of Charity was what Father Mullon had told her, that they came to New Orleans in 1830 and worked in the Poydras Orphan Asylum, where she found them. Then they moved into "Old Withers" in 1836. Now in 1838, the Sisters were to be in charge of a brand-new orphanage for girls. What progress they were making!

Subscription lists were opened, and Margaret headed them all. Parishioners and Catholics the city over contributed generously. Benefit balls, parties, and auctions were given by prominent people, raising huge amounts of money. Appeals were made for funds throughout the city.

A fair was held, at which arts and crafts and delectable edibles were sold. Margaret, the Sisters, and ladies of the parish fashioned elaborately dressed dolls, doilies, antimacassars, scarves, and decorative items, some of which were sold and others raffled. They embroidered little girls' dresses, tea towels, and face towels. Ladies who were not handy with a needle turned out pineapple upside-down cakes, iced muffins, and chocolate fudge—all of which were very popular. Still others made lemonade, root beer, and tea. The fair brought in huge profits.

And Margaret, daily pushing her milk cart, with Andrew at her side, advertised the need for funds for her orphans more eloquently than she advertised the quality of the milk and cream she was selling. She always came home with donations. Who could refuse a woman who labored long hours for no other purpose than to give to the poor and the orphans?

Money donations, all told, amounted to $36,000. Bishop Antoine Blanc made up the deficit of $7,000. The architect Dennis E. Hayden was contracted to build the orphanage in the 1400 block of Clio Street, and the construction began.

Whenever time permitted, Margaret took several of the little girls for a walk to the building site to see the progress of the house. They stood silently, awestruck, holding hands and watching. As the building took shape, they saw that it was to be three-and-a-half stories high, with dormer windows in the mansard roof. The second and third stories had balconies with floor-length guillotine windows for cross ventilation.

On the ground floor would be Sister Regis's office to the front and a huge dining room and dayroom to the rear. Upstairs on the second floor would be dormitories, and on the third, the residence of the Sisters and Margaret Haughery.

On February 16, 1840, six Sisters of Charity and 109 orphans (and Margaret) took possession of the new orphanage. With Sister Regis's permission, the children spent the day running around inside the building, ooh-ing and aah-ing, finding the cots with their names on them, and looking out the windows at the levee, where ships' masts, thick as a forest, bobbed with the motion of the water. They were enchanted.

Margaret, as thrilled as any child, took the hand of little five-year-old Lydia and made the tour of the building. Up

The New Orleans Female Orphan Asylum, 1404 Clio Street, built in 1840, on the lot donated by the Saulet-Foucher families. (Courtesy Waldemar S. Nelson)

and down the stairs they went, examining every dormitory and closet. Their tour ended at Lydia's cot.

"This is where I'm going to sleep, Margaret. Do you like it?"

"I think it's the most wonderful place to sleep in the world," Margaret said. The child giggled, hopping from one foot to the other, too excited to keep still. "You'll have all your friends around you, and when you wake up in the morning, they'll be the first ones you'll see. Won't that be nice?"

The child's eyes filled with tears of joy that spilled down her cheeks. Margaret sat on the cot and gathered the little girl in her arms, rocking her with a gentle motion. *This is why God sent me here,* she thought, *to give little moments of happiness to these unfortunate children.*

On the cold, brisk morning of February 20, 1840, the building was dedicated and placed under the patronage of St. Patrick. Then in 1843, the name was changed and the institution was incorporated as the New Orleans Female Orphan Asylum, to indicate that it was for the care of orphans from all over the city, not only from St. Patrick's parish. Despite this fact, the asylum soon became popularly known as the Camp Street Asylum. This was the female counterpart of the New Orleans Catholic Male Orphan Asylum on Bayou St. John, the first Catholic orphanage in the archdiocese, opened in 1834 by Father Adam Kindelon. Father Kindelon had been followed as pastor at St. Patrick's by Father Mullon.

The New Orleans Female Orphan Asylum received state appropriations from 1843, the year it was incorporated, until the eve of the Civil War, in amounts that averaged $4,000 a year. But without the charitable gifts of benefactors, it would have been impossible for it to function.

In 1845, a chapel was erected on the property for the needs of the Sisters and the children. Several prominent, wealthy families took up the cause, and the chapel went up within the year. It was a white frame structure, served by priests from the St. Louis Cathedral, St. Mary's on Chartres, and St. Patrick's on Camp.

A meeting was called by Bishop Blanc in May 1845 to propose that the Sisters open a school for Catholic children of the Second Municipality. The proposal was adopted.

In the beginning, the school was in the asylum, and outsiders were taught there with the orphans. Then in 1846, a house was rented on the corner of Clio and Prytania, the downtown corner, for use as a school. The building was later bought by the archdiocese for the school and used until 1860, when it was separated from the Camp Street Asylum and functioned as a parish unit.

8

St. Theresa of Avila Church

BY 1848, FAUBOURG STE. MARIE had grown so fast that Bishop Antoine Blanc realized that another parish was needed to serve its people. Furthermore, he wanted a permanent church, not a chapel, on the Saulet-Foucher property alongside the asylum. This was to be his next project.

Once again Margaret began her appeal for donations as she walked her route. Once again, benefit affairs were held. This time, a mammoth bazaar was staged by the people of the neighborhood from December 15 to 20, 1848, in which there were not only refreshments and arts and crafts to buy, but raffles, stage performances, and auctions.

Prominent Catholic laymen and friends of the asylum came forward with huge donations. And as always, Margaret helped to circulate subscription lists, her own name being at the top. The Catholic newspaper announced that pews in the new St. Theresa Church would be leased on and after December 1. The rush to reserve family pews was overwhelming.

In July of 1848, the bishop contracted Theodore E. Giraud to design the new church building to be erected at the corner of Camp and Erato streets on the same lot as the New Orleans Female Orphan Asylum.

A newspaper account of the period describes the church as a "Gothic church with unusual juxtaposition of Gothic form and detail." The cornerstone was laid in 1848 and the construction was completed in 1849 at a cost of $30,000.

Plans for the interior of St. Theresa of Avila Church, designed by Theodore E. Giraud, corner of Coliseum and Erato streets. Construction began in 1848. (Courtesy Rev. Teodoro Agudo, pastor)

The interior of St. Theresa of Avila Church, 1871. (Courtesy Rev. Teodoro Agudo, pastor)

St. Theresa's Church (1848) and Rectory (1915), corner Coliseum and Erato streets, c. 1915. (Courtesy Rev. Teodoro Agudo, pastor)

St. Theresa Rectory (left), St. Theresa's Church (center), The Louise Day Nursery (far right), c. 1930. (Courtesy Rev. Teodoro Agudo, pastor)

The interior of St. Theresa of Avila Church, Colisem and Erato, 1995.
(Photo by Tracy, courtesy Rev. Teodoro Agudo, pastor)

The church was dedicated on Sunday, December 9, 1849, by Bishop Blanc under the invocation of St. Theresa of Avila. The interior of the church with its beautiful stained-glass windows was breathtaking, indeed, but the ceremony was endless.

Margaret looked down the pew and her heart went out to the little girls, whose heads were nodding after three hours of blessings. First there had been a procession, followed by a blessing of the exterior of the church and a blessing of the interior of the church, after which Bishop Blanc had pontificated at a Solemn High Mass, complete with Latin hymns sung by a choir. Assisting His Excellency were fifteen priests. Two sermons were preached, one in French and one in English, and the words were not spared. The function began at 9:30 A.M. and was not over until almost twelve o'clock noon.

It was bitter cold that December morning, and the children were all shivering. Margaret wore her black dress, which she reserved for Sunday Mass and special occasions, and as always, her knitted shawl and bonnet. In honor of the occasion, the ladies of the parish had made for each child a new dress of sensible broadcloth, with braid or ric-rac trim, and each head was adorned with a dark bonnet that would serve, Margaret warranted, for many years.

A few stomach rumbles nearby reminded her that no one had yet had breakfast. They had been fasting from midnight to receive Holy Communion at Mass. Now, at last, Communion had been served and the Mass was ending.

After the procession of priests down the center aisle, Margaret and the children left the church to walk around the corner to the orphanage. Margaret held a child by each hand. They were all looking forward to the hot meal that a group of parish ladies had offered to prepare in their absence. Bishop Blanc and Father Mullon had been invited. This, of course, further delayed the removal of the little girls' "good dresses" and their well-deserved nap in their warm, cozy dormitory.

9

Yellow Fever Epidemic of 1853

A LOUD KNOCK AT THE KITCHEN DOOR startled Margaret as she was having her morning coffee. She glanced at the clock. Six A.M. Who could be here so early? Only she and Sister Regis ever rose before six o'clock.

"Come in," she said. The door was always open. There was no crime in the area. The door swung wide and she saw the face of her young Negro helper Andrew, a look of anxiety in his eyes.

"Good morning, Andrew," she said. "Why are you here at this hour?"

"Father Mullon," the boy caught his breath. "He send me to tell Sister Regis. He wonts her ta send five or six Sisters to nuss at de Char-ty Horspital. Now. Today."

"But why? What's goin' on?" Margaret asked. "Is it an epidemic?"

"I don't know, Miss Mar-gret. Das all Father tole me."

"All right. Help yourself to some coffee. I'll go talk to Sister Regis."

Margaret poured a cup of coffee for Sister Regis and added milk and sugar. She took the center hallway to Sister's office. The room was bright with daylight even so early in the morning. With its eastern exposure, it allowed light to pour in through two floor-length windows in the far wall. Sister Regis sat behind her desk, making use of the early morning quiet to look over her accounts, answer her correspondence, and make plans for future events before the day became too hectic.

Margaret put the cup of coffee on the desk. It was her morning ritual. "How's about ya, Sister?" Margaret asked. "Did ya sleep well?"

"Oh, yes." She looked up and smiled. "And you, Margaret?"

"Well enough, but Andrew came on the run a few minutes ago with a message from Father Mullon. You're t' send five or six Sisters to Charity fer nursin' duties t'day."

Sister frowned. She looked up at Margaret above her square glasses. "What's going on there?" she asked.

Margaret shrugged. "Don't know. Hope it isn't a yellow fever outbreak."

"Couldn't be. I read in the paper just a week ago that the city is disease-free. There hasn't been an epidemic in six years."

"Maybe I should go, too," Margaret said. "I'm a good nurse. I nursed my foster mother when she was ill, and my husband, God rest his soul."

"No, Margaret. Go with Andrew on your milk route. We need the money and the food you bring home. Besides, if it *is* the fever, you might come down with it."

"I don't think so," Margaret said. "I was with my mother and father and my sister Kathleen every moment before they died in Baltimore when I was nine, and I didn't get it then. I must be immune."

"All the same, you go on with Andrew. You're our provider, and that is where we need you."

Margaret nodded.

That May morning in 1853, pushing her cart with the huge milk cans alongside her young companion, Margaret suddenly felt very old. It had been seventeen years since she'd joined the Sisters and found her niche in the world. For most of that time, she'd been a dairy proprietress, now the owner of forty milk cows.

The animals were sheltered on a piece of land Margaret had purchased in an undeveloped area uptown. There, she had a staff of men who cared for them, milked them, and pushed carts like her own in other neighborhoods. All brought their money to her on Fridays and received their wages.

She thought about the investments she had made, putting her excess profits into stocks and bonds, which paid much better interest than the banks. It was all for the children when the need arose, and what was left when she died would be for them, too. She made loans to friends, as well, at fair interest rates, if they wanted to start a business or if their own businesses needed help.

For the first ten years, from 1838 to 1848, her earnings had gone into helping the orphanage pay off its debt. After that, her profits went to the church. But always, there was money for the orphans' upkeep.

Another one of her charities was Dr. Stone's Infirmary at Canal and Claiborne, where the Sisters of Charity had taken charge in 1845. It was called *Maison de Santé*. Dr. Stone had been a pioneer in the use of ether in Louisiana. The Sisters' excellent nursing care had gained such approval that many came for treatment there and larger quarters were needed. From Dr. Stone's Infirmary would grow another huge hospital staffed by the Sisters of Charity. It would be called Hotel Dieu.

Margaret was now forty years old. She had become such a successful dairywoman in the past seventeen years that dairymen came to her for advice and consultation. She took pride in that. But she realized on this hot May morning, as she trod along in her calico dress and her Quaker bonnet, that she was no longer a tender of the children, as she had set out to be, but a provider, just as Sister had said.

That saddened her. In the beginning, she used to dress the little girls for the day, and change them again for bed. She had fed the babies and changed them and rocked them to sleep when they were colicky. But now she was far removed from all that. She was an entrepreneur. Her own success had taken her away from the work she loved most.

Truth be told, she could have paid someone to walk her route with Andrew. But for Margaret, the route was and always had been a way of dropping hints to her customers about the needs of "her children" and a means of picking up leftover food and clothing in return. Only *she* could ask for cash donations and names on subscription lists when one building or another was under construction. Her customers would give all they had if *she* asked them. As a beggar, she was irreplaceable, and she understood that. It was God's will; He had put her here.

Her route was also her source of information on every subject. Her customers were her newspaper. From them, she learned everything that was going on in the city. She had never learned to read or write, though she memorized the shapes of words on street signs and in the newspapers; and she'd been forced to learn to write numbers and do rudimentary arithmetic. She had always meant to learn the right way, but it seemed there was never enough time.

Her customers told her about deaths in their families, about visiting relatives, construction going on, dignitaries coming to the city, everything. She didn't really need the newspaper. But no one had told her anything about an epidemic. Today she would ask them.

At the houses of Margaret's first four customers, the replies were the same. "No, we haven't read a thing about an epidemic. Sure an we'll say a prayer we won't be havin' one."

But at the fifth house, Mrs. O'Grady opened the shuttered front door and came out to sit on the stoop while Andrew ladled out two quarts of milk from the large can into her pitcher. Although she knew nothing about a yellow fever epidemic, her husband, who followed her out to the stoop, had heard a rumor.

"It seems an Irish laborer come in on an immigrant ship," he said, "an' the man was admitted to Charity Hospital about a week ago, the same day the article said the city was disease-free, if you don't mind."

"Well, what did he have?" Margaret asked.

"The black vomit. He died the same night."

"Oh, saints preserve us!" Margaret exclaimed, making the sign of the cross. "Well, why wasn't it in the noospaper?"

"The doctors ain't too quick to announce the beginnin' of the yellow fever season, y' see. They're afraid they might be wrong. It might be somethin' else, like malaria, and they'd be causin' a riot fer nothin'. Then they'd have the city officials on their heads fer discouragin' tourists an' businessmen from comin' here."

"But our *lives* might be at stake!" Margaret said in anger. "If ye'll pardon me, I think the health of everyone in the city should take first place in the minds of the councilmen."

"Sure an' I quite agree," said Mr. O'Grady.

That night, when the children were in bed, Margaret and the Sisters met in the dayroom. The nuns who had nursed that day seemed sober and serious.

"Another patient died today," said Sister Agnes, "and the Sisters will bear witness, the man's eyes were yellow, he was jaundiced, and he was sufferin' from the black vomit."

The nuns who had stayed at home gasped and their lips moved in silent prayer.

"*Another* patient?" Margaret asked. "Who was the first one?" She wanted to hear from Sister Agnes's lips the same information she had heard from Mr. O'Grady's.

"The first was an immigrant, too. They both came in on the same ship a week ago," the nun answered.

"Dear Mother Mary!" said Sister Regis, pressing her fingers to her lips.

Sister Agnes continued, "Doctor didn't trace the source of the fever when the first man died. But after the second one, he decided to look into it, and before we left, he told us they'd both come in on the *Augusta,* which arrived a week ago with more than two hundred immigrants."

Several nuns drew in audible breaths at this bit of information.

"It seems the *Augusta* had been in close quarr-ters with another ship, where several crew members died of the yellow fever while docked in Jamaica."

"Dear Lord in Heaven," Sister Regis said, "let's kneel and pray."

The yellow fever epidemic in Jamaica, they later learned, had swept through the island like a tornado, and a New York newspaper warned, two weeks before the *Augusta* docked in New Orleans, that the disease was being carried by sailors and dock workers to distant ports.

But New York was a long way away, and Jamaica was even farther. The people of New Orleans didn't know and didn't care. They were following the events of a sensational murder trial in the news. And then in June came word of a possible slave rebellion that never materialized. They had plenty to think about and talk about, without troubling their minds with yellow fever. It was an annual event, which would probably take few lives this year, if any at all.

Members of the "Can't-Get-Away-Club," merchants and tradesmen whose businesses kept them in town, commiserated with each other as their neighbors took off for country homes in Mandeville across Lake Pontchartrain or for cities along the Mississippi Gulf Coast. It was cooler there and disease-free, and summer getaways were commonplace, whether there were epidemics or not.

Those who remained in the city settled down to the unusual heat and the swarms of mosquitoes, "a barbarous horde of great, ugly, long-billed, long-legged creatures," according to one local paper.

In a city of 150,000 people, a total of 50,000 left town. Of the 100,000 that remained, approximately one out of every ten would die.

Within a week, the newspapers began announcing the numbers of deaths. Such news could not be kept secret forever. By July 2, the papers said 25 people had died of the fever. The following week, 204 more deaths had occurred. And by the middle of July, the total was 429. A second exodus of New Orleanians was under way.

"Why do we have so many epidemics?" Margaret asked Father Mullon. She had stopped at St. Patrick's Rectory along her route for a cool drink of water. "What is it about New Orleans?"

The priest frowned. "It's a port city for one thing. Anyone can bring disease in. There are no quarantine stations." He helped himself to a glass of water and sat facing Margaret at the kitchen table. "Then, too, it's the filth and squalor. That's what the new sanitay-tion department says. The gutters are filled with garbage and human waste, and the rains turn them into lakes of filth. That's what spreads cholera and malaria."

Margaret shook her head at the enormity of the problem.

"The people know all this filth eventually flows into the river," he said, "so they don't drink river water. They drink water from their cisterns. But that doesn't seem to be helpin', so we have t' wonder what's in the cisterns."

"Mosquitoes breed there, Father, that's for sure."

Father Mullon shrugged. There was much they didn't know about the fever that plagued them every summer to some degree, even if not to epidemic proportions. "Mayor Crossman has at last set up a municipal sanitation department, but it seems to be too late for *this* summer. We need more immediate measures now."

In the second week of July, Margaret decided she was needed at the hospital, and that's where she would go. She turned over her milk route to Andrew and whatever friends he could get to help him, with a promise of wages. She told him to keep the milk cans clean and to make the boys wash their hands several times each day.

"You're not goin' to the hospital, Margaret, and that's final," Sister Regis said, trying to be stern. "What would we do if you came down with the fever?"

Margaret looked forlorn. "You let the Sisters go, and they could come down with it."

"But that's different. They've offered their lives to God anyway."

"And I?" Margaret looked at Sister Regis, her eyes brimming.

The Sister's eyes welled with tears and the two women came together in a heartfelt embrace. "I'm sorry, Margaret. You've offered every minute of your life to God. If you want to nurse the sick, go with them. And God go with you all."

After that, Margaret left each morning with the nursing nuns to care for the sick and dying at Charity Hospital on Common Street. Walking to the hospital, they saw hearses rolling incessantly toward St. Louis Cemetery. The streets were deserted except for hearses. Returning in the evenings, they heard artillery being fired "to clear the atmosphere," and they smelled the smoke from hundreds of tar barrels scattered throughout the city, which sent up dense clouds of smoke and lit up the streets with an eerie glow.

At the hospital, they saw scenes that might have been in Dante's *Inferno*. Patients in filthy cots, on the floors, and spread out on the lawns in front of the hospital grabbed at their skirts as they passed and begged for water or for something to ease their pain. Others vomited black matter, and still others had no control of their bowels. The stench was overpowering.

Margaret and the nuns tried to comfort the patients as they passed, praying with them and holding their feverish heads as they vomited. Doctors, too few to make a difference, tried the time-honored cures of bleeding and purging, which were useless. Nothing succeeded.

As patients died, their bodies were carried out of the hospital and laid on the *banquettes* by men with gauze masks over their noses and mouths. Twice a day, the bodies were picked up by the death wagons, if they had not been claimed by the families. Often, so many were sick in a family, there was no one left to care for the dead. It was rumored that the bodies of the unknown dead were burned in a funeral pyre. Margaret didn't ask; she didn't want to know.

Nursing yellow fever victims was especially difficult for Margaret. Whenever she looked into the jaundiced face of a middle-aged man, she recalled her dear father breathing his last. A woman's cries of pain brought back to mind her mother's last agony, even after all these years.

She also went with the nuns to the homes of victims too ill to be taken to the hospital and nursed them there. By August, all activity at the orphanage had ceased and every available nun was on nursing duty. By the first week of August, two hundred people were dying each day in the city.

The Sisters shared their greatest grief when five of the twenty-two nursing nuns died in the epidemic. But Margaret survived.

Many couples died, leaving small children alone at home. The Sisters took the abandoned children in their arms and comforted them. Then, exhausted and heartbroken for the little ones, they took them by the hand and led them to their new home in the asylum.

10

After the Epidemic, Life Goes On

WHAT AMAZED MARGARET was that throughout the terrible nightmare summer months of 1853, life with its many detailed activities went on, in some places as if the people knew nothing about the yellow fever epidemic.

Before the plague descended upon the city, the New Orleans port was flourishing, and its citizens were heady with optimism. Sailing ships were lined up five-deep at the docks and the wharves were jammed with merchandise. Goods were brought in from the heartland of America and shipped out to ports half a world away. In the French Quarter, shops and cafes were opening almost as you watched. The Garden District, upriver from Faubourg Ste. Marie, was becoming the setting for sprawling mansions built on grounds a city block wide.

Everywhere Margaret went, money was changing hands. It was the "American" century in New Orleans, people said. The aim of American merchants was to carry on unrestricted trade with the thought of expansion and more expansion, and ultimately, amassing great wealth.

Now in the mid-century, the character of the city streets of New Orleans began to emerge. Houses with hipped roofs, galleried cottages, and earthen *banquettes* with wooden curbs began to take on the "look" that would be New Orleans. In the second quarter of the century, when Margaret had arrived, brick two-storied houses and business places began to crowd out and outnumber the smaller Creole cottages. Greek Revival architecture reached its zenith in popularity, and by mid-century, the city had more Greek architecture, some said, than Athens in its prime.

In the very last days before the epidemic began, on May 10, 1853, the greatest specimen of Greek Revival architecture was dedicated on Nyades Street (St. Charles Avenue) at Lafayette Square. It was the Second Municipality Building, which became at once the City Hall Building, since the three municipalities had rejoined into one city for the benefit of all. The detail of the magnificent building designed by architect James Gallier, Sr., was "sure t' take yer breath away," as Margaret put it.

A ride on the omnibus, the street railway car that ran along Nyades Street (later, the St. Charles Avenue streetcar line) cost one bit (half a quarter). The American theaters were very popular, as was the French opera. Entertainment was a must in the cosmopolitan, fun-loving city.

When the New Basin Canal was completed in 1838, trade thrived in New Orleans as never before. Merchants, whose commission houses lined Triton Walk (Howard Avenue) between the New Basin Canal and the river, were said to be doing business on an avenue of gold.

Margaret was not unaware of this great wealth. She begged from these merchants without shame, knowing the wealthy powerbrokers would fold large bills into her hand, perhaps to have her end her story quickly so they could get on with their business. But Margaret didn't care why they gave, as long as they gave.

Then came the epidemic. It was remarkable to note that those who did not fall ill with the disease went on about their business, tried to make a living, cooked meals, cared for their children. Some never saw a single person die, never held a sick victim in their arms. Amazing, Margaret thought.

She had seen so much of death and dying, scenes of horror that would invade her dreams for years to come. It was hard to accept the fact that life went on. Yet, when she and the Sisters came home from the hospital at night, they had the children to take care of, to play with and pray with, and to put to bed. In this, they saw some semblance of normality in their lives. It was a badly needed emotional restorative.

Margaret often thought of the hundreds of passengers on the *Augusta* that had arrived with the first two seamen to die of yellow fever in New Orleans. What had happened to all those poor souls who had been on their way to the New World with visions of a free, happy life? Had they all succumbed to the fever?

The papers called yellow fever a "Strangers' Disease." This, Margaret came to understand, meant that it affected new people in the area, like recently immigrated Irishmen and Germans and their families. People who were born in New Orleans and grew up here had a kind of immunity to the disease.

Two recent epidemics in 1847 and 1849 had apparently immunized the children in the asylum. Not one of them came down with the fever, although Margaret and the nuns who cared for the sick came home to the children each night. Many of the city's children, however, were orphaned by the epidemic. In 1853, 209 children were admitted to the New Orleans Female Orphan Asylum, and it was now splitting at the seams.

For a time, during the epidemic, when ships had stayed away from the port, there was a shortage of food and other necessary items. But the minute the first cold snap broke the fever in the fall, natives knew the danger had passed. Contact with those who had had the fever was no longer feared. Women volunteers came out of their homes to nurse the sick back to health in the hospital, and the nuns were relieved for a badly needed rest.

Ships soon appeared on the riverfront again, their network of rigging discernible from the children's dormitory windows. Business resumed, more brisk than ever before, and the horrors of the epidemic were forgotten.

St. Vincent Infant Asylum, 1507 Magazine, on the corner of Race Street, which opened in 1858. In this more recent picture, the Daughters of Charity and children line up along the sidewalk. (Courtesy Sally Schreiber)

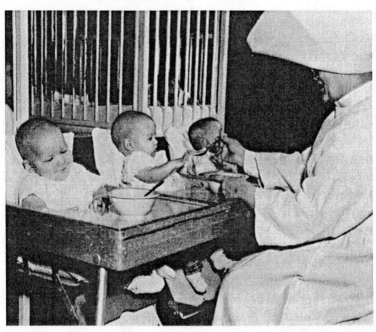

A nun feeds three babies at once at St. Vincent's. (Courtesy Sally Schreiber)

11

Institutions of Daughters of Charity Grow in Number

COMPELLED AT LAST by the overcrowded conditions at the Camp Street Asylum (New Orleans Female Orphan Asylum, also called St. Theresa's), Sister Regis made a move she had been contemplating for a very long time: a division of the orphanage population according to age. It was an idea ahead of its time. Sister Regis was a pioneer in the field of special methods for institutional childcare.

The immediate problem in 1853, however, was the convalescence of the children who had fallen sick with yellow fever. They were sent to recuperate in a small, frame house in the town of Carrollton that had been bequeathed to the Sisters of Charity in 1847 by Father Augustin de Angelis. Besides the house, he also gave the nuns several vacant lots alongside it.

The orphans were so numerous that the Carrollton house was not large enough and additional temporary buildings were constructed on the vacant lots. The Howard Association sent forty children whose parents had died from the fever. The Portuguese sent more. And the city authorities sent still more. An additional house was rented for the children, and more Sisters were sent to care for them. In 1854 there were fifty orphans in what became known as St. Mary's of Carrollton. It remained in operation until 1869 when it was so badly in need of funds, most of the girls were sent to St. Elizabeth's. It was later abandoned and became a tenement. It was torn down in 1938.

Generous donations were made for the care of these children. Margaret, as always, gave as much as she could without selling investments that would later bring in interest for future donations. So, for the time being, the pressing problem of housing the additional orphans was solved.

Sister Regis had long been determined to subdivide her orphans. She wanted to prepare her teen-age girls to support themselves when they left the shelter of the asylum. This meant they must be given separate facilities to develop their natural talents and learn a useful trade. They knew how to read and write and do simple arithmetic. Now they must learn a way to make a living.

In 1852, before the epidemic, Sister Regis received her first appropriation of $6,000 from the state for this project. She was ready to move. She announced at the board meeting of the Corporation of the New Orleans Female Orphan Asylum in March of 1853 that Mr. Philip Rotchford, a friend of the Sisters, had obtained a lot at Magazine and Josephine. Their long-desired project for the older girls would begin as soon as funds were available.

The teen-age girls were ecstatic. At last, they were being recognized as grown-ups who would soon be on their own. They preened at their own importance. Margaret and Sister Regis nudged each other, amused at their pleasure in simply growing up.

In 1855, the teenagers moved into the *first* St. Elizabeth's in the 2000 block of Magazine Street, an extension of the New Orleans Female Orphan Asylum. Dr. William Newton Mercer, an Episcopalian, gave $5,000 toward the new building. This institution was called St. Elizabeth's for the patron saint of his daughter, Miss Elizabeth Mercer.

Dr. Mercer, an army surgeon who came to New Orleans after serving in the War of 1812, lived in a home on Canal Street designed by the noted architect James Gallier, Sr. (This home is today's Boston Club.) Dr. Mercer promised a yearly donation to St. Elizabeth's, and after his death, a legacy.

Sister Angela Murta and two Sister companions opened the new asylum with twelve orphan girls. Since St. Mary's of Carrollton was overcrowded immediately after the epidemic of 1853, the older girls at the Carrollton home also began returning to the new St. Elizabeth's on Magazine Street. There they labored as their numbers grew, until 1871, when their establishment was moved to a more suitable location on Napoleon Avenue.

The home was first called St. Elizabeth's House of Industry. It was self-supporting, its income derived from the needlework, fine washing, millinery, cooking, housework, and other industries practiced by its young women. As time passed, the House of Industry built up a clientele. It was the first industrial school in the South under Catholic auspices.

Mr. Philip Rotchford opened a subscription list, which, through his zealous efforts, brought in $6,000. The girls over fourteen went to St. Elizabeth's for five years. Each girl, upon entering, was given three outfits of clothing.

If Sister Regis had been vexed with the problems of the teen-agers, Margaret had always been troubled by the need for a separate home for the infants and young children under seven.

"The babies need their own home, too," she told Sister Regis.

"How well I know it," the Sister replied. "They need special care and handling, and by people who know what they are doing." But in a practical vein, she asked, "But where is the money to come from?"

"Partly from me," Margaret said. "I have a good bit saved. I could have Mr. Rotchford keep an eye open for a good location." She raised her eyebrows in supplication.

"Margaret, Margaret, what would we have done if God hadn't sent you to us?"

"What would *I* have done?" Margaret asked.

Sister Regis held another meeting of the Corporation of the New Orleans Female Orphan Asylum in March 1858.

She explained why it was entirely unsatisfactory to keep infants and older girls together in the same asylum. She asked that a new building be found for children under seven. The motion was carried.

In November 1858, a small house was found at 1507 Magazine, at the corner of Magazine and Race. It was to be called St. Vincent Infant Asylum, commonly referred to as St. Vincent's. Margaret called it her "Baby House." On November 5, 1858, thirty babies from the New Orleans Female Orphan Asylum were transferred to this new home, along with three of the Sisters.

Later, arriving from Emmitsburg, Maryland, Sister Michaela Devine took over as permanent administrator. With her were Sister Mariane Brennan and Sister Mary Louise Schneider. The infant asylum received instant public approval, and by the end of 1858, donations of $1,180 had been received and seventeen more infants had been admitted.

With these changes, the complete subdivision into three groups was being effected: the older girls at St. Elizabeth's House of Industry, the intermediate girls at the New Orleans Female Orphan Asylum, and the infants to seven-year-olds at St. Vincent's.

One Sunday Margaret heard the new pastor at St. Theresa's, Father Bellier, denouncing "the bigots" in his energetic way. Later, she asked Sister Regis what "bigots" he was referring to.

"There's a political party, Margaret," she said. "They call themselves the Know-Nothings, or sometimes the American Party or the Nativists. They're tryin' to prevent immigrants from voting or holding political office. That's all I know."

Margaret frowned. She knew the Irish were looked down upon by the Creoles. She knew they were considered only one rung up the social ladder from Negroes, slave and free, especially since they vied with them for jobs cleaning streets and stevedoring and doing the most menial labor.

Most Irish immigrants, like those who came to dig the New Basin Canal in the 1830s and the immigrants who were victims of the potato famine in the late 1840s, knew nothing but farming. But there were no farms in New Orleans. It was a port city, and an immigrant was not likely to become a successful commission merchant overnight. They had families to feed, usually big ones. So they took whatever work they could get. They were loud-talking, true enough, and eager for an argument, but was it fair that they were all considered hooligans?

Although Margaret had seen signs posted in business places saying "Irish Need Not Apply," she had never heard of bigots who were out to do bodily harm to the Irish. But she was to have personal knowledge of this hatred.

One morning when she and Andrew were pushing their milk cart, a man stepped out from behind a wagon and threw stones at them. One of the stones struck Margaret just above the eye. She reached up with her right hand and when she looked at it, she saw blood. She turned to face the aggressor.

"Get off the street, you shanty Irish cow," he called out to Margaret, "and take your little nigger friend with you. Quit beggin' from decent folks. Stay out of our way, or there'll be hell to pay, I can tell you."

Margaret saw that the man was backed up by three large thugs. She would not have approached him in any case. She looked at Andrew and nodded. They turned their cart around and went back home, while the stranger and his companions laughed and made rude remarks.

For the next few weeks, either Father Mullon or Father Bellier accompanied Margaret and Andrew on their rounds, at least in the neighborhood where the men had insulted them. Soon they were on their own again, the incident forgotten. But the air of hatred for all immigrants remained, especially for the Irish, who made up twenty percent of the population by the end of the decade.

In numbers alone, they were a threat. And because they were largely illiterate, they stood out in stark contrast to the Creoles of the French Quarter, who considered themselves aristocratic and cultured to their fingertips.

An Irish organization had been formed in 1836 called the Ancient Order of Hibernians, a division of a national organization of the same name, whose purpose was to protect the Irish people and most especially their religious buildings, which seemed to be the target of the Nativists' contempt. It had never been needed more than now.

"Did you know that in New York City," Father Mullon told Margaret, "the Hibernians made a human chain around St. Patrick's Cathedral, not only as a sign of protest, but to protect the building so it wouldn't be put t' the torch?"

Margaret's jaw dropped. She had never heard such a thing in her life. Then, remembering threats against their own St. Patrick's Church she had heard along her route, she said, "It might not be a bad idear if we would do the same."

Soon after Margaret's frightening experience, she was blessed with an event of unsurpassed joy. She knew that her brother Thomas, one of her older siblings who had remained behind in Ireland when the family emigrated, had come to Baltimore in 1849. In January of 1852, she had received a letter from him saying he was in Baltimore, that he had a wife and family, and that he was financially unable to make a trip to see her. She dictated a letter to Father Mullon to send back to him, enclosing money. She wrote him another letter in April of 1852, again sending money. This she continued until he told her he was no longer in need of her assistance.

At last, in 1857, he wrote to say he would be coming for a
visit. Margaret was beside herself with joy. She told the
Sisters, and a flurry of housecleaning was done in anticipation of his arrival. On Margaret's advice, he came to St.
Vincent Infant Asylum to look for her. When Margaret and
Thomas laid eyes on each other, after a separation of more
than forty years, they were overwhelmed with emotion.

"My dear Thomas," Margaret said.

"Margaret," was all Thomas could utter.

They embraced tearfully, unable to believe they were at last
reunited. Laughing and crying at the same time, they hugged
joyously. Then they backed away to look at each other.

"I would have known you anywhere, Thomas darlin',"
Margaret said, brushing a tear aside. "Ye're the very spittin'
image of me." She laughed. "'Tis like lookin' in the mirror,
fer sure."

"True fer you," Thomas said.

There was so much news to catch up on, they didn't
know where to begin. After introducing Thomas to the
nuns, who were waiting impatiently, Margaret took her
brother to a private salon and they talked for a very long
time. Thomas told Margaret how everyone had sufferd at
home from the potato famine in 1846 and how he and his
family, along with thousands of others, came in cramped,
unsafe ships over the ocean to America. He told how good
their Uncle Matthew had been to the three oldest children,
rearing them like a kindly father. He said their sister Mary
had stayed behind in Ireland even through the famine, and
she was still living in Tully.

Margaret related to Thomas the sad details of the deaths
of their parents and their baby sister Kathleen all those
many years ago in 1822. She told him of the loss of his
younger brother. She told him of her marriage and the
death of her husband and child. At last, Thomas understood the many sorrows that had visited his sister in her life
in America.

Then quickly, Margaret told him how happy her life was now with the orphans and the Daughters of Charity. She said she had been singularly blessed by God with peace of soul that had long ago healed all her heartaches.

In the days that followed, Margaret showed her brother around New Orleans. She introduced him to her many friends and benefactors of the orphans. Then, tearfully, they parted once again.

As the decade came to an end, talk about abolition seemed to be on everyone's lips, taking precedence over talk about the Know-Nothings. The subject of freeing the slaves was argued along the riverfront and among Margaret's friends and customers.

Few of these people were wealthy enough to be slaveowners, so it was not their own property they would be fighting to protect. But the sugar and cotton plantations upriver and down, worked by Negro slaves, had made the port city prosperous. This industry indirectly put food in the mouths of stevedores and merchants. None of them wanted to change the system.

Shiploads of hundreds of bales of cotton crossed the wharves of the city daily, to be sent by commission merchants to manufactories in the North, where the cotton was processed into cloth. Much of it was sent as raw cotton to Europe, especially to England. Sugar raised and processed in Louisiana had many markets in Central and South America, as well as along the Eastern seacoast.

Margaret, like many kind-hearted white citizens, had mixed feelings about slavery. She believed that all men should be free, and that slavery was a wicked insitution begun before she was born by greedy, evil men. But, she wondered, if all the slaves in the South were freed today, where would they go? What would they do? Who would take care of them?

She and the Sisters owned slaves, Andrew among them, but never was a teen-age boy more gently treated. He had clothes, food, a warm place to sleep, and rewarding work to do. He loved working with Margaret, and when given the chance to take charge of her dairy uptown, adamantly refused the offer. Andrew was loved, not only by Margaret but by all the nuns, and his integrity reflected the gentle care he had received.

She turned her head to look at him now—a gangling, barefoot, light-skinned Negro—and wondered how he might survive if he were freed and set off on his own to find his way. Margaret cared for him as much as she cared for the children in the orphanage. He was one of her charges.

In the 1850s, Margaret had been approached for loans several times by a man named D'Aquin, who owned a bakery at 74-76 New Levee Street (later, South Peters). Each time, she advanced him a loan and in return, received stock certificates in D'Aquin & Co. Her intention was always to help the man get back on his feet, but there came a time in 1859 when she owned more stock in the company than he did, and she was faced with the option of taking over the bakery or letting the man go into bankruptcy, thereby losing all the money she had advanced him. It was a difficult decision. She spoke to Father Mullon.

"Father, how can I take over a bakery?" she asked, a troubled frown appearing between her brows. "Sure an' I know nothin' a-tall about runnin' such a business."

"But Margaret," the priest argued, "if you don't buy it, you stand to lose a great deal of money."

"And if I *do* buy it, I'll have t' sell the dairy. I can't possibly run two big businesses at once. Besides, I'll be needin' the money from the sale of the dairy to buy the bakery."

"Then sell it. The time is right. I don't think it will be too much longer before the property owners in the Garden District will be complainin' about cows in their backyards."

"You're right, Father. It's the right thing to do. But the

bakery's a failin' business. If Mr. D'Aquin can't make a go of it, how in the world can I?"

"I believe in you, Margaret. You have good business acumen."

Margaret raised her eyebrows. "Acumen?" she asked.

Father Mullon laughed. He never got by with a fifty-cent word when talking to Margaret. "Good business sense. Look at the success you made of the dairy, and you knew nothin' about cows."

Margaret smiled. She wanted to buy the bakery. It was a challenge. "I'll do it," she said, feeling as excited as one of her teen-agers.

Margaret had her friend, Charles Macready, an attorney, handle the transfer of both properties. The proceeds from the sale of the dairy went toward the purchase of the bakery and the necessary renovations and improvements. Now that she was into it, she wanted it to be the best bakery in the city.

She consulted the most progressive bakers in New Orleans. She learned that although no one had used steam yet in operating a bakery in the South, it was the coming thing. She decided that while she was making improvements, she might as well go all the way and install the very best equipment.

To her delight, there was an apartment above the bakery, where she could live close to her business. She would be rising early every morning, if she wished to provide people with bread for breakfast. But rising early was nothing new to Margaret.

The apartment was small, but it was the first time since Charles died in 1836—now twenty-three years ago—that Margaret would have a place of her own. She would furnish it simply, with little more than a bed and a chest and a rocking chair.

She still had only two daytime calico dresses (one on, and one off being laundered) and a black bombazine for

Sundays. She still wore her Quaker bonnet for which she was known. She would not have changed her image now. She was a good businesswoman—hadn't Father Mullon said so?—and she wanted to present a recognizable and trustworthy image. Now, more than ever, she would need to be a *superb* businesswoman, God help her!

This advertisement ran in a Carnival parade paper in 1880, when Margaret was still running the bakery.

A drawing of the Little Sisters of the Poor from A Little History of the Little Sisters. (Courtesy Mother Christine)

12

The Dairywoman Becomes a Baker

AFTER SUPPER IN THE NEW Orleans Female Orphan Asylum, a
week after Margaret had officially bought the bakery, when
all the girls were still at the dinner table, Sister Regis
touched her fork to her water glass to get attention. Silence
descended over the room.

The Sister stood up. "My dear little girls," she said, "I
have something to tell you." She sighed, finding it difficult
to find the words. "I'm afraid we aren't going to have our
dear Margaret with us anymore."

The youngest girls began sobbing and were soon followed by the middle-school children and at last by the teen-
agers, who sometimes joined them for dinner. The sobs
became a wail, and Sister Regis saw the children lowering
their faces to their hands in sheer distress. What had she
said? She went over her words in her mind.

"Wait! Wait!" Sister Regis urged. She looked into dozens
of pairs of watery eyes. "I don't mean that she's ill or dying."
Small smiles began to replace the frowns on the young
faces. "I just mean she's not going to be living here with us
anymore."

The wails began again, now louder than ever. Sister Regis
looked at Margaret. She mouthed the words, "You tell
them."

Now Margaret got to her feet and began to walk around
the large dining room as she spoke. "Now listen to me, all

you dear, sweet angels. Nothin' terrible is happenin'. In fact, somethin' wonderful has happened t' me, and I want t' share it with you."

Now she had their attention.

"I've bought a bakery," she said, clasping her hands before her bosom, "where I'll soon be makin' bread an' cakes an' crackers an' so many other good things." She smiled and they smiled back, a bit uncertainly. "'Tis only a few blocks from here. After school, I know you'll be allowed to come in small groups, with an older girl in charge, to visit me." She looked at Sister Regis, who nodded vociferously.

"But where will your bed be?" asked curly-headed, five-year-old Suzanne.

"It will be in the little apartment just above the bakery," Margaret answered, taking the child's hand. The wails began again. "Now, now, ya see, I *must* live there because I'll be gettin' up early in the mornin' to start makin' the bread. But you can come see my apartment, a few at a time. It isn't big. An' once you see me bed and the chest where I keep me dresses, an' ya look through me upstairs winder, sure an' you'll be able t' think of me there. And I'll come and visit you here when I can. We'll still be together."

Everyone seemed mollified, if not totally happy. Margaret suddenly realized that she had been sleeping in the same house with the orphans for twenty-three years. She had been there when they awakened in the morning and there when they went to bed at night. She belonged to them, in the truest sense of the word. All these children, seated in varying age groups before her, were accustomed to her being there, as part of their family, and she couldn't bear to give them heartache.

"I have another good idear," Margaret said. "The teen-age girls are learnin' trades so they can make a good livin' when they leave the home." Margaret never said *asylum* or *orphanage*, always *home*. "Some of the teen-agers might want t' be trained t' work behind the counter in me bakery, sell-in' bread and cakes."

"Oh, *I* do," said Megan, raising her hand.

"Can *I* go?" asked Carrie.

Margaret locked glances with Sister Regis, who nodded. "We'll give you turns behind the counter," Margaret said, "and decide who will work there on a permanent basis."

Now the teen-agers were all smiles, talking among themselves about starting to work in the world at last. And with Margaret!

Within the week, Margaret had her bed, chest, and rocking chair transferred from the orphanage to her apartment. Those three pieces of furniture would have been sufficient to satisfy her Spartan tastes, but the teen-age girls, eager to give her a gift and put their skills to work at the same time, made white cotton curtains for her windows and a bedspread of a patterned fabric to dress up her little room. They brought her plants in small colorful pots for her windowsill and crocheted scarves for her chest of drawers. The best gift came later, an oval rag-rug the girls took months to make, which gave a warm, homey feeling to her apartment.

The children's visits were the most pleasurable moments in her new life. But as renovation of the bakery progressed, Margaret was soon working from dawn to sunset, and there was little time for visiting. She was no longer their tender. She was now a provider only, with little or no contact with her beloved children.

Within weeks, the steam machines for operating the ovens had been installed, and with their overhead levers and pulleys, they were a miracle of speed and efficiency. The building had to be enlarged to allow for the new machinery, and renovation was in progress for several months.

Margaret experimented with a variety of crackers, putting them on trays for her customers to sample. She asked what they liked best, and then she decided which ones to list in her advertisements.

In the 1870s, with the help of an artist, she designed an ad that ran in the *Times-Democrat*, showing her three-story building with its wrought-iron balcony on the second floor and two wagons in the street outside bearing the name, Margaret's Bakery. The ad read, in large letters, "MARGARET'S STEAM AND MECHANICAL BAKERY." And in smaller print, "Fancy and Extra Fancy Crackers of all Varieties and Brands. Soda Crackers, Cream Crackers, Picnic Crackers, Navy Bread, Pilot Bread, Ginger Bread." The list was endless.

The ad said that these goods could be packaged in tin cases of five, ten, twenty, and twenty-five pounds for foreign shipment. Now with a capacity of processing 300 barrels of flour a day, Margaret was prepared to receive large orders.

Her business thrived. Within a year, it was one of the most successful in the city. Perhaps she did have business "acumen," as Father Mullon had said. She smiled to herself at the word. In time, the building extended from 74 to 78 New Levee Street (South Peters Street), and back to the next parallel street, which was Commerce.

She was proud to own an establishment that turned out "the staff of life," a product she could give the poor. One of her particular charities was The Little Sisters of the Poor, who, like Margaret, begged for the poor.

The Little Sisters arrived in New Orleans in 1868, when Father Ernest Lelièvre, a 41-year-old priest of the Congregation, was sent from France to prepare for the homes of the Little Sisters in the United States. In New Orleans, they settled in what is now 1501 North Johnson Street, where they remained for 104 years, until they moved to the Mary Joseph Home in Algiers in 1972.

From 1868 on, they stopped by Margaret's Bakery regularly, and Margaret filled their wagon with rounded loaves of bread, which they in turn brought to the old people of

the city. In the 1860s and 1870s, Margaret provided half the
old people in the city with bread. She also gave the Little
Sisters of the Poor a twelve-vault tomb on St. Paul Avenue
in St. Louis Cemetery No. 3. (To date, 58 Little Sisters have
been put to rest in that tomb.)

She sent fresh bread daily to the orphans, and when "her
children" visited, she gave them lemon cream biscuits and
iced sugar cakes and sent them off with large tins of sugar
cakes for the other children.

Margaret, in 1860, at forty-seven years old, was the owner
of the only steam bakery in the South. Her profits enabled
her to give even more to the orphans. She amassed a con-
siderable fortune. She had to admit to herself that although
she had never worked toward that goal, she was now a very
wealthy woman.

She worked six days a week, closing the bakery only on
Sundays, when she dressed in her black dress and Quaker
bonnet and joined the children at St. Theresa's Church for
Mass. She had dinner with them on Sundays and spent the
afternoon with her friend Sister Regis. They talked about
business and children and plans, always plans.

Margaret wanted no recreation or diversion from her
work. The closest she came to resting was a period of an
hour or so each afternoon when she sat in her rocking
chair in front of the door of her bakery, wielded her pal-
metto fan, and talked with customers, friends, and passersby.

Many important businessmen of the city got out of their
carriages to greet her. Barthélémy Lafon, the architect/sur-
veyor/philanthropist, always took a moment to get out of
his rig, approach her with great respect, and shake her
hand.

"How well you're lookin', Miss Margaret," he said. "Hard
work and success sure agree with you."

She smiled at his kindness. "You're lookin' well yourself,
Monsieur Lafon," she said. "Won't you come in for coffee

Margaret is visited by neighbors as she sits in her rocking chair outside the bakery in the late 1870s.

and sample a new cream cake I've just put on the market?"

The stream of visitors was endless, many coming to ask her advice on a matter of business or tell her their problems. She had become a beloved, respected entrepreneur in a city of entrepreneurs.

After her first year in business, Margaret had forty workers in her shop: bakers who knew good recipes, mechanics who kept her steam equipment in order, drivers, salespeople, and bookkeepers. And Andrew, her jack-of-all-trades, worked wherever she needed him. Her bakery had become big business. Margaret thrived on it. She recognized in herself the ability to match wits with the craftiest wholesalers and suppliers. As she liked to tell Father Mullon, she wasn't Irish for nothing.

Among her customers in the early 1860s was a young man she very much admired named Bernard Klotz. In time she hired him to work with her while he was waiting to get called up by the army.

To Margaret, he was like a son. She could depend on him to manage the bakery when she had to run a business errand, without fear that everything would fall apart in her absence. And when he had to make a business decision on his own, it always seemed to be the right one. She loved the young man and determined to leave the running of the business to him when she died. She did not legally adopt him, but she made it known both to him and to the Sisters that after her death, he would be in charge. She did not have the slightest doubt that he would continue the charitable work she had begun, giving bread to the orphans and the poor.

She missed "her children" however. Often, as she lay in bed at night while she said her rosary, she stopped to picture one little face or another. How soon they were all grown and gone, married or working on their own. Many who had come to the orphanage as toddlers were long since married and operating successful businesses. They had passed through her life and given her enormous joy. But now she hardly saw them anymore, except for the few who worked behind the counter and were usually too busy to stop and chat about how things were "at home."

She had become a baker; a tycoon, some would say. Her success had been her undoing. As a provider, she could do more for the children, but only from a distance—not on a personal level. She no longer had daily contact with them. That was her personal misfortune.

13

Crossing Enemy Lines, Locking Horns with Major General Butler

"D' YA THINK LOUISIANA WILL SECEDE from the Union, Father?" Margaret asked.

"Not if they can help it," Father Mullon said.

"Oh? Y' mean they aren't for keepin' slavery, then?"

"It has nothin' to do with slavery in our case, Margaret. New Orleans needs the food and the manufactured goods that come downriver from the North. We have no farms and no industry here. If our port is blockaded, the city could be starved out."

Margaret's eyes grew wide. She hadn't stopped to realize it, but what the priest said was true. And if they *were* blockaded, how would she get her flour?

They were seated inside the bakery in a small office Margaret had arranged for prospective clients. She had furnished it with a settee and an easy chair. Andrew had brought them coffee, and Father Mullon was sampling one of Margaret's new cakes.

"My flour comes from the Midwest," she said thoughtfully. "I suppose if there's a war, that would be enemy territory."

"Sure an' it would be."

"Saints preserve us! We're all Americans. We all need to work and eat and . . . live."

"That's the horror of war, Margaret," Father Mullon said. "It changes every aspect of your daily life." He sipped his coffee. "And it's especially hard if you're fightin' against your own people."

"Maybe it won't come to that, Father."

"Let's pray it won't."

But it became reality. Abraham Lincoln was elected president in 1860. He said he favored non-extension of slavery. The handwriting was on the wall. Everyone knew that eventually he would see that it was wiped out altogether. In January 1861, Louisiana seceded from the Union.

Travelers began returning home before the war began. Gen. P. G. T. Beauregard, the Creole darling of New Orleans, resigned his post at West Point and returned to his native city, where he met with Maj. Gen. Mansfield Lovell, who was now in charge of Confederate troops in the city.

One day, Margaret saw the Louisiana Zouaves drilling in the Place d'Armes in front of the St. Louis Cathedral. She knew a bit about them because Bernard's friend was in the Zouaves. They were the First Special Battalion, Louisiana Division, and their uniforms were modeled on the French infantry units' in North Africa and the Crimea in the 1850s. Organized by Roberdeau Chatham Wheat, the Louisiana Zouaves were known as Wheat's Tigers or the Louisiana Tigers. In their scarlet fezzes and baggy Moroccan trousers, they looked like costumed play soldiers at drill rather than a grim contingent of men getting ready to battle the enemy to the death.

On April 12, 1861, the Confederate forces under General Beauregard took Fort Sumter from the Union in a bitterly contested battle. The War had begun. Soon afterwards, a blockade was thrown up around New Orleans, and by the fall of 1861, the docks lay silent and empty. Stevedores had no work. Mail did not go through. People were starving. Yet in the Vieux Carré, Adelina Patti was singing in the new French Opera House, starring in *Lucia de Lammermoor*. New Orleans was a city of contrasts.

The Yankees, they heard, were on the move, taking towns

and beseiging cities. Gold and silver were disappearing from the market, and Confederate paper money was the chief medium of exchange. Margaret tried to keep her prices down, and for those who had no money at all, her bread was free.

She opened a small coffee shop, which was in truth more of a soup kitchen, where drifters and old people could stave off hunger with a hot cup of soup. It became a gathering place for beggars and derelicts who roamed the waterfront. Margaret's bread was always free to the poor. But if she had the slightest inkling they might sell it to buy whiskey, she cut the loaf in half and gave them both halves, with a wink of the eye.

In the first year of the war, New Orleanians who joined the Confederate army were sent to Virginia, and only the militia remained to protect the city. No one expected an invasion from the mouth of the river, which was fortified by the old Forts Jackson and St. Philip. But in April 1862, news sheets passed to the waiting crowds outside Newspaper Row on Camp Street proclaimed that Flag Officer David Farragut's flotilla was coming upriver from the Gulf of Mexico.

When Margaret heard the news, she took her bread wagon down Camp Street to see what was going on. "Wait 'til they get to Fort Jackson and Fort St. Philip!" someone in the waiting crowd shouted. "We'll give 'em 'what for.'" Everyone cheered the arrogant speaker. Other news sheets said that Major General Lovell had announced that when Farragut reached the forts, all Confederate troops would be evacuated from the city, for "no enemy would bombard an undefended city."

Until Farragut's activities in the Mississippi, the city had seemed as far removed from the actual fighting as if it were on the moon. But then on April 24, 1862, Farragut's flotilla broke through the boom that spanned the river between the two forts. Within two hours, the Federal navy was steaming northward toward New Orleans.

No newspaper had to tell them when cotton and tobacco were being burned on the riverfront. The scorching, acrid smell permeated the city.

On that very night, Margaret was sleeping fitfully, her nostrils filled with smoke from the riverfront. She kept dreaming that an oven of bread had caught fire and the loaves were burned to a crisp. While she was tossing and moaning in her sleep, a knock at her door awakened her. Now fully awake, her eyes smarting, she rose to answer the door.

Framed by the doorjamb was Andrew, who had come with a message. "Miss Mar-gret, it's about Sister Regis," he said, as he turned his hat around and around in his hands.

"Well, what, Andrew? Is she ill?"

"No, Miss Mar-gret. She daid." He lowered his head. He hated to be the bearer of such news.

Margaret pressed her hand to her mouth as tears came to her eyes. "But how? When?" she asked. "No one told me she was ill."

"She wasn't ill, Miss Mar-gret. She jes' pass on in her sleep. Das all." Andrew looked up to meet Margaret's brimming eyes.

Of all the grief Margaret had known in her life, for her parents, her sister, her husband, and her baby, none had been as hard to bear as what she felt at this moment for her dearest friend and companion of the last twenty-seven years.

"Wait downstairs, Andrew," she said, talking past the painful lump in her throat. "I'll dress an' be right with you."

In the wagon ride to the orphanage, Andrew coughed on the smoke in the area of the riverfront. "Is the fire gettin' close, Miss Mar-gret?"

"It won't spread, Andrew. They're burnin' cotton an'

tobacco on the riverfront so the Yankees won't be able to sell 'em." She could say no more. Her heart was filled with sorrow.

Two days later, Sister Regis was buried in St. Louis Cemetery No. 2 in a large vault of the Daughters of Charity, where eventually Margaret herself would be buried. Sister Regis was laid out in the new headdress of the nuns, called a carnette, a large, white, starched bonnet resembling a sail.

The nuns were no longer called Sisters of Charity. In 1855, they had been incorporated in the Daughters of Charity of St. Vincent de Paul. *So many changes!* Margaret thought, as she grieved for her dear departed friend. She made it known then and there that she was to be buried alongside Sister Regis, who had been truly her sister in spirit, as well as her most beloved friend.

For several days, no word was heard of the occupation of the city or what it would mean to the citizens. Then, on May 1, 1862, Maj. Gen. Benjamin Butler arrived in the city to take control as Commander of the Department of the Gulf. New Orleans was a city under seige.

One of Butler's first orders was the hanging of William Mumford, the local gambler who had torn down the American flag from the United States Mint on Esplanade Avenue. This rash act of rebellion had frightened and thrilled every citizen, happening as it did even as Farragut's flotilla was lined up in the river a block away.

The order was swiftly carried out, and Mumford was hanged in front of the Mint. The general was known thenceforth as "Beast" Butler. But in spite of the hanging, the people of the city did not buckle under. They remained defiant.

"Margaret, I saw it with my own eyes," Mary Lafferty said, standing behind the bakery counter making change. She nodded good-bye to the customer and turned to Margaret.

"Two ladies were walkin' down the street, an' comin' toward 'em were two Yankee officers in their fancy blue duds. Well, the ladies slowed their pace as they got near the men, and then, without a how-do-you-do, one of 'em spat at one of the officers." She nodded her head for emphasis as Margaret's jaw dropped. "The man had to take out his handkerchief and wipe his face."

"Well, what had the officer said to her?"

"He hadn't said a word. They were mindin' their own business, those men were," Mary said. "Now Butler's got the Woman Order out. It's in the mornin' paper." Margaret nodded. She didn't like admitting she had never learned to read. It diminished her image as a businesswoman. "He's givin' his officers the right to treat any New Orleans lady as a street walker, plyin' her trade." Mary turned to wait on the next customer.

Margaret could not believe her ears. She had seen many Union officers on the street. They had done nothing but bow to her or tip their hats. It was lunacy for New Orleans' women to fly in the face of defeat.

But Margaret was to wage her own personal battle with Butler. For the first year of the war, she had supplied Confederate soldiers with bread. Then after the occupation, the remaining military forces had been dismissed from the city.

Margaret soon learned that although the city of New Orleans was under occupation, the towns across Lake Pontchartrain were not. It was through those channels that she could obtain flour for her bakery. There was only one obstacle: Getting there meant crossing enemy lines and possibly being arrested and thrown into jail. She chose to ignore that little detail and sent Andrew and a group of male workers to the cities on the Gulf Coast by land in several wagons big enough to handle many barrels of flour. So far, they had managed to slip through enemy lines undetected.

But when the Fourth Louisiana Regiment was brought captive to the city, she piled her cart high with loaves of bread and marched through the enemy pickets herself. She was determined to get into the prison to deliver bread to "her boys."

"Sorry, Miss," a young Union private said. "You ain't allowed to cross these lines."

She flicked her reins against her horse's rump as if she had not heard the young man. Again he told her to halt. At last, Margaret got down from her wagon and, with the strength she had inherited from her O'Rourke forebears, she seized the sentry in her arms and set him out of her path before he knew what was happening to him. She then got back into her wagon and moved through the lines. No one else tried to stop her.

The incident was reported to Butler, and she was ordered to come to his office in the St. Charles Hotel. Margaret asked Father Mullon to go with her, fearing her punishment might be along the lines of poor William Mumford's. She trembled as she sat outside the office of the Beast, but when she was ordered to enter, she squared her shoulders and lifted her chin in the air.

After they had been announced, Margaret and Father Mullon were asked to take a seat. Butler cleared his throat and addressed Margaret.

"Miss Haughery," he said.

"Just Margaret," she replied.

"Miss Margaret. Surely you know you have broken our rules about crossing enemy lines. Our soldiers were too gentlemanly to restrain you physically, but I understand you did not return the favor." He appeared to be restraining a smile.

Margaret pursed her lips and then spoke. "The Confederate prisoners are hungry men, General. I have never turned away a hungry person in my life."

"So I have heard," Butler said.

"I'd feed your own soldiers if they were hungry. In fact, I've done so already, on one or two occasions."

"I've heard that, too," he said. "And because you had the foresight to include in your generosity the hungry on both sides, you will be allowed to cross the picket lines to obtain your flour from the Gulf Coast towns. I'll give you a pass with my own signature, which will be good for as long as I'm commander here."

"Thank you, General," she said. The words stuck in her throat, but she forced herself to say them because she knew so much depended on his goodwill.

Now he turned to Father Mullon, and Margaret had a chance to study the general. He was an ugly man, so wall-eyed that she didn't know which eye to look into when she addressed him. He was bald, except for a ring of hair above his ears that had been allowed to grow long to his shoulders. And to make matters worse, he was fat. The overall effect was comic, a fact that had not been overlooked by local political cartoonists.

"And you, Father Mullon," he said, "have caused me much perplexity. You have espoused slavery and fought against me, praying surreptitiously for Confederate victories."

"No, you're wrong. I do not espouse slavery," Father Mullon answered. "'Tis wrong, but abolition is not the answer. It would result in the exploitay-tion of thousands of Negroes after they are freed." He paused, gathering his thoughts to counterattack. "Slavery has a parallel in the North with bigotry and Nativism and child lay-bor in sweat-shops. Most slaveowners I know treat their slaves like members of their own families. I wish you'd have a chance to talk to Margaret's Negro helper, Andrew. He'd tell you his experience as a slave."

"I'm sure there are exceptions."

"Many," the priest said. "And you spoke of surreptitious prayers. We pray for an end to hostilities. I share the emotion of most Southerners, who feel that their land has been laid waste by intruders who started a blood bath. Each person prays according to his conscience. This cannot be regulated by proclamations."

"It has also come to my attention that you refused burial to some of our Federal soldiers."

"Not because they were Federal soldiers," Father Mullon replied. "They were fallen-away Catholics and could not be buried on sacred ground. Figuratively speaking, sir, I should like nothing better than to bury the whole Federal army."

Margaret wanted to applaud or to laugh, but she forcibly held her pride in check.

Butler smiled a one-sided smile. He walked back to sit behind his desk once again. He looked weary and despondent. "Your people are captured," he told the priest, "but they have not surrendered. They are conquered, but not subservient. I have restored order to your city, punished crime, brought provisions to your starving people. Yet my soldiers have been subjected to reproach and insult. Can you do nothing to control your rebellious people, Father Mullon?"

Father Mullon felt proud of the stand his people had taken. Yet, knowing subservience was the wiser course, he said, "I will try." Then after a pause, he added, "It is not entirely in my hands. You give me too much credit."

After they left Butler's office, Margaret, with her pass to cross enemy lines clutched tightly in her palm, said, "I know you won't agree with me, Father, but I don't think he deserves the name of 'Beast.' He's doin' his job. Maybe he hoped t' make an example of Mumford. Maybe our people would be a lot *more* rebellious if he *hadn't* hanged Mumford."

Father Mullon nodded. It was probably true.

In spite of the war, in 1862 the Daughters of Charity purchased a site at 1314 Napoleon Avenue and in 1863, opened a wood-frame school called St. Joseph's Institute. This school replaced an 1855 institution called the House of the Five Wounds, which subsequently operated at the site that would later be DePaul's Hospital.

In 1865, the Daughters commissioned architect/builder Thomas Mulligan to build a new brick building for St. Joseph's in the middle of the Napoleon Avenue site. In 1868, after the war, the Daughters moved the school to the 2100 block of Constance Street and renamed it St. Mary's Parish School.

In 1871, they established a branch of St. Elizabeth's Home in the former school building at 1314 Napoleon. Two years later, St. Elizabeth's was established as a separate institution from the New Orleans Female Orphan Asylum. Then in 1873, the Napoleon Avenue location became the main campus for St. Elizabeth's, and the Magazine Street location became a branch, to be torn down the following year.

In 1880, Albert Diettel designed a major addition to the original school building on Napoleon. In 1883 a wing was added on Perrier Street, according to Diettel's design, and a mansard roof was added to the original building. The building was again expanded with the Prytania Street wing.

Meanwhile, in 1864, the year before construction began on the new St. Elizabeth's, another project was in progress for the Daughters of Charity, even while Federal military forces still controlled the city. It was the building of the permanent home of St. Vincent Infant Asylum. Space was badly needed, for once again, children were being left without parents or with only one parent, due to fatalities on the battlefield.

Much of the work on St. Vincent's was done by free black men, many of whom were artisans. The Federal government considered the institution so important that it paid the labor costs.

The Daily Picayune of September 23, 1864, said: "The

debris of the old farmhouse, which has been used as the St. Vincent Infant Asylum, has been removed and the foundation laid for a commodious and suitable home for the helpless infant orphans."

In December 1864, it said: "The cornerstone was laid for an impressive group of red brick buildings, designed by Thomas Mulligan . . . the fine cast iron gallery on the front and the interesting courtyard in the rear opening from Race Street."

Appropriations were received for the care of the children from the federal, state, and city authorities. From time to time, the Sisters purchased additional lots of land on the same site. And although the whole South was impoverished, people of all classes helped with donations to complete the structure in 1867.

In 1869, the wing was completed to care for expectant mothers. Married, unmarried, patients of means, and charity patients were all cared for in the St. Joseph's Maternity Wing of St. Vincent's. Then in 1870, a third building, first used as the laundry and stable, finished that group of structures so familiar to New Orleanians even today.

Margaret was, of course, one of the outstanding benefactors of the home. She not only furnished bread without charge for years, but also made one substantial donation after another, giving even her bakery plant and her life insurance to St. Vincent's. In 1866, she defrayed the cost of glazing the entire building.

There are such interesting donations in the records as these: In 1867, $100 from Father Duffy, $200 from Mr. Macready, and $500 from Margaret Haughery. In 1873, Margaret gave $3,010.91; in 1875, she gave $1,167 and cancelled a bread bill of $1,346.85. The saddest donation was her life insurance policy, which came to the Daughters of Charity in 1882 after her death. It was in the amount of $3,725.67. Also in her will was the land, building, and machinery of Margaret's Bakery, at 74-76-78 South Peters

Street, which she estimated in her will to be worth $30,000.

By 1870, the New Orleans Female Orphan Asylum needed to provide a safe and comfortable boardinghouse for young businesswomen who earned modest salaries, including the young ladies who had completed their training at St. Elizabeth's industrial school. Following the Civil War, there were also many working mothers who needed day care centers for their children.

It was decided that a second building would be constructed directly behind the New Orleans Female Orphan Asylum building, obscured from view from Clio Street. The handsome, three-story building was sandwiched between the original orphanage and St. Theresa's Church. Margaret contributed money as always and solicited donations from others for the new building, which would be called the Louise Home, in honor of St. Louise de Marillac, cofounder of the Sisters of Charity in 1633.

With two large buildings, the Sisters were able to accommodate working ladies in the old building and a day care center in the new. A wing was added to connect the two buildings on the Prytania Street side, so that young ladies living in the old building, when going out for the evening, could pass through the door of the Sisters' residence in the new building before leaving, in that way respecting the custom of chaperonage that existed in most good family homes.

14

Margaret's Death:
The End of the Legend

ON A MONDAY MORNING IN 1881, when Bernard Klotz entered the bakery, he was surprised that Margaret was not behind the counter, getting her change box ready. He asked the bakers who arrived earlier if they had seen her. No one had. Becoming fearful, he rushed upstairs to her apartment and knocked at the door.

"Come in," she said in a weak voice.

With a frown of apprehension, Bernard hastily entered and approached her bed. In all the years he had worked with Margaret, which now numbered almost twenty, he had never known her to lie abed on a workday morning after seven o'clock.

"Margaret," he whispered as he took her hand. "What is it? Are you ill?"

"It seems so, me boy, but I'll be well soon." She squeezed his hand gently. "'Tis nothing major. Don't make a lot over it, Bernard."

Bernard pressed his palm to her forehead. "You're burning up," he said. "I'm going to get Dr. Stewart. I'll take your rig and have him back here in no time. Now you just stay in bed. I'll send Mary up to look after you." He stopped at her door to look back. "Now promise you won't get up."

"I promise," she said obediently.

Now he was really worried. Margaret would not give in to

111

herself unless she was really ill. And if she promised to stay in bed, well . . . God only knew how sick she really was.

The doctor was soon at her bedside checking her temperature and her pulse. He listened to her heart with his stethoscope and made her cough so he could hear if there was rattling in her lungs. "Tell me exactly how you feel, Margaret," he said.

"I feel weak, Doctor. Very weak."

"Are you in pain?"

"I have a terrible headache."

It was the first time Bernard had ever heard Margaret complain of pain. It had to be excruciating.

The doctor put both hands to the back of Margaret's neck and lifted slightly. Margaret moaned. "You may have a kind of grippe that's going around. Sometimes patients get headaches with it." He spoke to Mary Lafferty, who had come up when Bernard left to get the doctor. "Please close all the shutters and make it as dark as possible in here and bring up an ice pack for her head. Make it two. One for her forehead and one for the back of her neck."

Mary nodded. "I'll go down and fix them now."

He turned back to Margaret. " I want you to rest in bed all day, and take only liquids. I'll leave you some headache powders. Take one right away." He poured water from her bedside carafe and held her head while she took the powder. "I'll pass back here this evening on my way home."

"Thank you, Doctor," Bernard said.

On the way downstairs the doctor asked Bernard, "How old is your mother now?"

"She's sixty-eight, but she's a very strong woman—at least until now. I've never seen her take to the bed before. I'm afraid she must be very ill."

The doctor smiled and nodded. "We'll know more by this evening."

"She isn't really my mother, you know," Bernard said. "She's sort of adopted me, but not legally."

The doctor nodded again. He knew that. Everyone knew everything about Margaret; her life was an open book.

Days passed, but Margaret did not get better. Some days were better than others. When she felt well enough and her head did not throb, she dressed herself and came down to try to work. But by ten in the morning, she would be back in bed, moaning with the pain in her head.

She ate hardly anything, and Bernard could see her growing thinner every day. Dr. Stewart called in another doctor for consultation, and while they both agreed that the headaches were an indication of a more serious problem, they could make no diagnosis. She was in and out of Charity Hospital for tests, always returning with no improvement.

At last, the Sisters prevailed upon her to take a private room at their own Hotel Dieu Hospital, which had opened in 1859. There she would get constant supervision, especially from the nuns themselves, and if specialists were called in to run tests, it would be so much easier for her.

Margaret went into the hospital and was there for many months, but her condition was beyond what the doctors knew how to treat. She grew steadily worse and suffered great pain with headaches. Her vision often blurred and she became dizzy.

She had many visitors in the months she was in the hospital, people who wanted to thank her for favors she had granted them in her lifetime. They knew she was a dying woman and their time to talk with her was growing short.

General Beauregard came by to wish her well. "'Tis sad," she said, "that you couldn't be recognized as a wartime hero 'til the Yankees left the city."

"Thank you, Margaret," Beauregard said, sitting at her bedside. "It did seem they were here for a very long time."

"What did they stay around for, General?" she asked. "Fourteen years! Didn't they know the war was over?"

Beauregard laughed. "Yes, Margaret. They knew. I'm

sure the soldiers all wanted to go home, too, but they had their orders."

Margaret closed her eyes and winced with the pain in her head.

"I'll leave you now, Margaret," Beauregard said. "I don't want to tire you. I just wanted you to know I'm praying for you."

"Thank you, General."

Another day it was Barthélémy ("Thomy") Lafon, the quadroon surveyor/philanthropist whom Margaret had so wanted to meet when she was first walking her milk route.

"Thomy," she said, "did you see the beatiful crucifix Pope Pius IX sent me?"

He glanced at the silver image on the ebony cross in a place of honor on her bedside table. "It's beautiful, Margaret," he said.

"Sure an' it's hard to imagine such a thing," she said. "You know how much that dear man must have on his plate, runnin' the Church all over the world. How did he find time t' bother with a nobody like me?"

"You're not a 'nobody,' Margaret. You're better known than you think. Even to the Pope, as you can see."

Margaret looked up into the jet-black eyes of her visitor. "I'm glad your people are free now, Thomy," she said sincerely.

"I know you mean that, Margaret." He locked glances with her. "For some of them, it's been a blessing. Others have known only grief. They've roamed the South like pitiful beggars and some came back to their former owners lookin' for work." He shook his head. "A change like this could take a century of adjustment."

"True for you," Margaret said. And then in a weak voice, she added, "I'm glad my dear friend Father Mullon didn't live to see what went on durin' Reconstruction." She sighed, weary with pain. "He would've hated to see Negroes an' whites an' carpetbaggers fightin' each other in the streets." She sighed again. "Do you think all that is over now, Thomy?"

"Oh, yes," he said. "I'm sure it is."

Margaret closed her eyes in death on February 9, 1882. She was sixty-nine years old. Her death certificate was signed by Dr. Jacob H. Wiendahl and the cause of death was shown as mental cancer.

The front page of *The Daily Picayune* ran a lead article enclosed in a black border on February 10, 1882. It read:

"A great calamity has befallen the orphans and the poor of New Orleans, the death of Mrs. Margaret Haughery, which sad event occurred last night at a quarter to twelve o'clock. Surrounded by kind and loving friends, she quietly passed away, exemplifying how wonderfully a beautiful life can make peaceful its termination."

On the editorial page of the newspaper were the words:

"She never had upon her hand a kid glove, she never wore a silk dress, though she earned by hard labor many thousands of dollars. But no woman has been borne to the tomb within the limits of New Orleans who was more generally respected and loved."

The funeral was held on February 11, 1882, at St. Vincent Infant Asylum. Thousands followed the procession down Magazine Street to Julia, then to St. Patrick's Church on Camp Street. Father Hubert, her confessor and friend, delivered the eulogy to crowds packed to the doors. Out on the street for a block or more were men with heads uncovered and women holding prayer beads and sobbing into their handkerchiefs.

In her lifetime, Margaret had been a laundress, a beggar, a dairywoman, and a baker. Yet, when she died, her funeral cortege was led by the mayor of New Orleans, and two former governors of Louisiana were among her pallbearers.

Be it Remembered, *That on this day, to-wit: the Eleventh of February in the year of our Lord One Thousand Eight Hundred and Eighty Two, and the One Hundred and Sixth of the Independence of the United States of America, before me,* **JOSEPH JONES, M. D.,** *President Board of Health and Ex-Officio Recorder of Births, Deaths and Marriages, in and for the Parish of Orleans, personally appeared:*

J. F. Callico a native of La residing at corner St Louis & Robertson Streets who hereby declares, that Mrs. Widow Margaret Haughery (White) a native of Baltimore, Maryland, aged 68 years departed this life, on the ninth instant (9 February 1882) at # 76 South Peters Street, in this city Cause of Death Omental Cancer Certificate of Dr. J. H. Steindahl.

Thus done at New Orleans, in the presence of the aforesaid J. F. Callico as also in that of Messrs. H. Kohlhaase & I. H. Lanauze both of this City, witnesses, by me requested so to be, who have hereunto set their hands, together with me, after reading hereof, the day, month and year first above written. O H Lanauze

J. F. Callico

President Board of Health and Ex-Officio Recorder.

The death certificate of Margaret Gaffney Haughery, 1882.

She could neither read nor write, yet during her lifetime, including what she bequeathed in her will, she left what is estimated at a half-million dollars to the orphans and the poor.

Among the mourners were rich and poor, people of every race and creed: William J. Behan, mayor of New Orleans; Governor Samuel D. McEnerny; former Governor Francis T. Nicholls; former Mayor Joseph A. Shakspeare; Bernard Klotz, her "adopted" son; prominent businessmen; members of the Chamber of Commerce; officers of the Mississippi Fire Company No. 2, of which she was an honorary member; and eleven separate groups of orphans.

All stores, commercial places, and city offices were closed for the day out of respect to her.

She was buried in a 24-vault tomb of the Daughters of Charity of St. Vincent de Paul in St. Louis Cemetery No. 2, where her friend, Sister Francis Regis Barrett, had been buried in 1862.

The tomb was later damaged in the hurricane of 1915. It was demolished in 1920. All remains were removed to St. Louis Cemetery No. 3, lots 21, 22, and 23 in Square No. 3. Margaret now lies in an unmarked grave.

Margaret's last will and testament was filed for probate in the Civil District Court for the Parish of Orleans, on Monday, February 13, 1882, by Messrs. Thomas Gilmore & Sons, attorneys. It had been written October 12, 1881, four months before her death, and notarized by William Joseph Castell, notary public for the Parish of Orleans, State of Louisiana, and duly witnessed.

In it she gave her maiden name, the name of her husband, her child, and her parents, all of whom were deceased. After two personal bequests, she began her list of gifts to charity:

I give and bequeath unto the Little Sisters of the Poor three thousand dollars.

I give and bequeath unto the Catholic Boys' Orphan Asylum, Third District of this city, three thousand dollars.

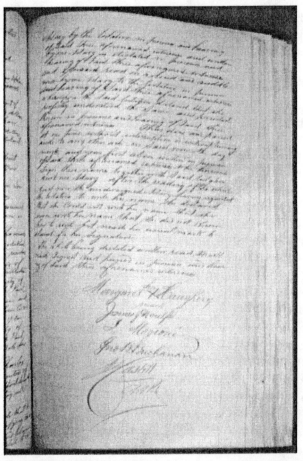

Last page of Margaret Haughery's will, showing her mark (X).

I give and bequeath unto the German Catholic Orphan Asylum the sum of one thousand dollars.

I give and bequeath unto the Seventh Street Protestant Orphan Asylum the sum of one thousand dollars.

I give and bequeath unto Widows' and Orphans' Jews' Asylum the sum of one thousand dollars.

I hereby liberate, cancel, and remit all amounts due me by the St. Elizabeth Orphan Asylum in favor of said St. Elizabeth Orphan Asylum.

I consider that I have about thirty thousand dollars invested as capital in the bakery establishment of M. Haughery & Co., and the residue and remainder of all I may die possessed of, in movables and immovables, rights and credits, I give, devise, and bequeath unto the Daughters of Charity of St. Vincent de Paul, Emmitsburg, State of Maryland, for the use and benefit of its St. Vincent Infant Asylum, corner Race and Magazine Streets, in the City of New Orleans, hereby instituting said Society of the Daughters of Charity of St. Vincent de Paul, Emmitsburg, State of Maryland, my sole heir and universal legatee.

In her will, she appointed the executors of her estate and revoked all other wills and codicils previously made.

At the bottom of this document were the words:

[The testatrix] declared she could not write her name, that she never wrote her name, that she did not know how to write, but made her usual mark to stand for her signature. The whole being dictated, written, read, mark made, signed and passed in presence and hearing of . . . three . . . witnesses.

[Original signed]
her
Margaret *(X)* Haughery
mark
James J. Woulfe
J. Magioni
Jno. B. Buchanan
W. J. Castell, Notary Public

End papers used by Klotz Cracker Factory. The name was sold with the business in 1892. The bakery continued well into the 1950s. (Courtesy Sheila Larmann)

15

The Bakery, Her Legacy;
The Statue, Her Pedestal

Margaret's Bakery After Her Death

Margaret left the management of her bakery to her foster son, Bernard Klotz. Strangely enough, she never legally adopted him and she did not mention him in her will. During her lifetime, they were closer than many biological mothers and sons, and he named his little girl Margaret in her memory. Nevertheless, she willed the bakery to the Daughters of Charity.

After her death in 1882, Klotz operated the bakery, leasing it from the Daughters of Charity (according to records in the Notarial Archives). The Robinson Atlas Map of 1883 shows the property listed as Margaret's Bakery, at 74-78 South Peters Street (by 1883, New Levee Street had been renamed South Peters Street). The City Directory shows it as Klotz, Bernard & Co.

In 1888, Bernard Klotz built his own bakery at 75-83 South Peters Street, across the street from Margaret's. Klotz's Bakery went into bankruptcy in 1893, when both the business and the name of Klotz passed into the hands of an attorney named W. C. Benedict. In the years that followed, this property changed hands several times, suffered losses from a fire on September 29, 1903, and had its street numbers changed to the present ones they are today. But in 1935, the telephone directory listed Klotz's Cracker Factory at 615-25 Tchoupitoulas Street, where it had turned up once again.

Now as for Margaret's Bakery, after her death, the records at St. Vincent's show that $200 a month came to the asylum from the bakery as rent or lease money. This was paid by Bernard Klotz to the Daughters of Charity, to whom she had bequeathed the establishment for the use and service of St. Vincent Infant Asylum. St. Vincent's records show that there was a fire in Margaret's Bakery in 1892, a fire which destroyed the building. How heartbroken Margaret would have been to see her precious bakery, which she had taken over with such trepidation and made into such a thriving business, go up in flames! But if Margaret were watching from heaven, she saw that from the ashes of the bakery rose five new stores, the rent from which paid one-fourth the cost of operating St. Vincent's. So Margaret must have smiled down on these establishments. If she were still alive, even her great business "acumen" could not have prevented the fire; nor could she have provided for her Baby House more adequately. She had done well when she willed her property to the Daughters of Charity. But Margaret's Bakery is no more, except in books like this or on very old maps.

Margaret's Statue

At Margaret's funeral, it was suggested that a statue be erected in her honor so that future generations of children might glimpse the image of a woman who had walked the streets in her Quaker bonnet and calico dress while selling milk and begging and who had bestowed all her worldly possessions upon the orphans and poor of New Orleans. The suggestion was enthusiastically supported.

Donations came to St. Theresa's Church and to all the orphanages Margaret had helped fund. In only two years, a sum of $6,000 had been raised and the statue was erected.

The sculptor Alexander Doyle, a native of Baltimore, then living in New York, was commissioned to do the statue. Doyle also sculpted the statue of Robert E. Lee standing on a pedestal in Lee Circle. Doyle examined a portrait of Margaret done in 1842 and then studied a photograph taken of Margaret much later in life. After talking to her most intimate friends, he fashioned a clay mold and sent it to Italy, where it was reproduced in white Carrara marble. Its pedestal is a block of sculpted marble on a seven-foot granite base. The inscription reads simply MARGARET.

The statue was placed in the center of a triangular park in front of the New Orleans Female Orphan Asylum. The park is bounded by Clio, Camp, and Prytania streets.

When the orphan asylum had been built in 1840, Margaret requested that the City Council purchase this triangular plot and make it a playground for the children. The Council had refused. But when the statue was erected in 1884, the Daughters of Charity owned the tiny park. The City of New Orleans purchased it back from the Daughters of Charity and made it "Margaret Park."

The statue was unveiled July 9, 1884, in the presence of hundreds of orphans from eleven institutions, with former Governor Francis T. Nicholls making the dedication. Margaret Park had been landscaped with palms, and the statue was set against the backdrop of the New Orleans Female Orphan Asylum and the Louise Home. The steeple of St. Theresa's Church was to the rear, adding its own beauty and dignity.

Governor Nicholls proclaimed, "The substance of her life was charity; the spirit of it, truth; the strength of it, religion; and the end, peace—then fame and immortality."

For many years, Margaret's statue was thought to be the first erected to a woman in the United States. Early in the twentieth century, however, it was learned that another had preceded it. The first was that of Mrs. Hannah Duston, in Haverhill, Massachusetts, erected in 1873, just a decade

This postcard from 1908 shows Margaret's statue as it sat in front of the New Orleans Female Orphan Asylum. Just to the left behind the orphanage, you can see part of the Louise Home. Beyond that is the steeple of St. Theresa's Church.

The Margaret statue in Margaret Park with the steeple of St. Theresa's behind it. (Photo by Tracy)

before Margaret's statue. But Mrs. Duston's act of bravery that precipitated the raising of the monument happened almost two centuries earlier.

On March 15, 1697, Mrs. Duston, mother of twelve children (and still bedridden with the last), her nurse Mary Neff, and her new baby, were taken as prisoners by raiding Indians who killed twenty-seven people in Haverhill and captured thirteen more to be sold to the French at Quebec for handsome bounties. (The father had herded his other children to safety in the village.) Two weeks later, Hannah's baby was killed, its head bashed against a tree because it was impeding flight from a vengeful posse.

At midnight, Hannah, her nurse, and a fourteen-year-old male prisoner killed a dozen Indians as they slept and ran to freedom in Haverhill. Her descendants erected a monument to her memory on Contoocook Island in the Merrimack River, just north of Concord, where the deed took place.

It might be appropriate here to mention the third statue erected to a woman, or more precisely to several women. In 1924, in Washington, D.C., a monument called *Nuns of the Battlefield* was unveiled. It immortalized several nuns, each in the habit of her respective order, who gave themselves over to the care of wounded soldiers during the Civil War.

Margaret's Portrait

An oil portrait of Margaret was made in 1842, when Margaret was twenty-nine years old. It shows the fresh complexion of the peasant Irish woman in her Quaker hat. In her bonnet and shawl, she holds two children nestled close at her sides. Painted by New Orleans artist Jacques Amans, the portrait is in the Roger Houston Ogden Collection. It was the highlight of the Irish-American Exhibition at the Presbytere April 6–May 14, 1995.

This is the photograph of Margaret taken later in life. Her statue is patterned more after this photograph than after her earlier portrait. (The Historic New Orleans Collection, Acct. No. 1989.14a, b.)

Margaret's Photograph

Mrs. William Frances Scheyd donated to the Historic New Orleans Collection a dramatic photographic portrait of Margaret. The photographer is unknown. The photograph is in an ornate period frame with the paper label of the framer, Laurent Uter, No. 38 Royal Street. He was at this address from 1875 to 1881. In the photograph, she wears the same shawl as that depicted in the statue.

Margaret

By Danny O'Flaherty

Each time, as I pass you by and whisper soft your name,
Those thousand little children, they must have felt the same.
You're the "angel of the Delta," and the "bread lady" too.
You gave your whole life, Margaret, to the orphans and the poor.

Chorus:
I would have loved to know you, but that was long ago.
I would have loved to talk to you, or maybe say hello;
But your memories still linger to this very day.
We will always love you, Margaret, in a very special way.

Your cart along the cobblestones, up the Channel way,
Down to the old French Market,
Making rounds of your dairy trade.
In a calico sunbonnet, you wore a threadbare shawl—
Saying, "Just call me Margaret"; sure you didn't mind at all.

Danny O'Flaherty, owner of O'Flaherty's Irish Channel Pub in the Vieux Carré, was reared in Connemara and the Aran Islands. When television was bringing the twentieth century into his village, threatening to destroy centuries of Irish tradition, Danny, through his music, helped keep alive the stories of an ancient culture and a simpler time. (Photo courtesy Danny O'Flaherty)

Daughters of Charity break ground for the new Hotel Dieu Hospital in 1920. Note the carnette caps that so distinguished them from all other orders.

Daughters of Charity outside the 1404 Clio Street complex composed of two buildings, the boardinghouse for young ladies and the day care center, in the 1930s. (Courtesy Waldemar S. Nelson)

16

After Margaret's Death:
The Charities Continue

St. Vincent Infant Asylum

After Margaret's death, funds were raised by fairs, concerts, dramatic presentations, a Magic Lantern Entertainment in 1888, a Stereoptican Exhibition in 1889, lawn parties, and a whist party in 1915—each reflecting the amusements of its era.

We see the same names recurring among donors, such as Mr. McKenna, who bequeathed a $25,000 legacy; Mrs. Denegre, who always made her home available for functions and gave sizable donations herself; Patrick Bourke O'Brien, who donated a square of ground containing 26 lots bounded by Palmyra, Banks, Lopez, and Rendon streets valued in 1884 at $1,000, but fifteen years later, at $10,000; Mme. Schreiber, who, after 1880, always supervised the dressing of the Christmas tree and the purchase of useful and amusing Christmas gifts for the children.

The Sewing Circle, started in 1898, and St. Vincent's Branch of the Sunshine Society (begun during the 1918 influenza epidemic) rendered notable service. The purpose of the Sewing Circle was to make clothes for the children of the orphanage.

The Elks, the Knights of Columbus, the *Picayune* employees and the *Times-Democrat* employees all helped in fund drives and contributions, so that the Sisters might care for an infant population that ranged for years from 170 to 200 children.

In 1917 there was an influx of babies due to World War I. A new nursery had to be opened and the porches on the old building screened. After a cry for help in the *Times-Picayune*, $3,000 was raised.

Noted physicians, surgeons, and baby specialists down through the decades gave their services free, matching the services of the Sisters. The state and city governments also provided appropriations.

The first Community Chest (now United Way) drive was held in 1925. Many asylums were funded by this drive, including the Louise Day Nursery, New Orleans Female Orphan Asylum, and St. Vincent Infant Asylum. No longer would these homes have to depend on uncertain methods of fund-raising for their operations. Now they would have the assurance of annual budget fund assignments.

In 1926, the Board of Catholic Charities changed its name to Associated Catholic Charities of New Orleans. In 1938, it became Associated Catholic Charities of New Orleans, Incorporated.

By 1958, the centennial of St. Vincent's founding, 25,000 children had been housed, fed, dressed, and loved in St. Vincent's. And the list of benefactors continued to grow. The St. Louise de Marillac Guild, the Louisiana Society, League of St. Jude, Adoptive Couples Together, Pius X Sodality, the East Jefferson Key Club, St. Vincent Guild, and scores of others gave time and money for programs of service provided at St. Vincent's. A century after its founding, St. Vincent's was still offering care and guidance to unwed expectant mothers. At that time their administrator was Sister Berenice.

By 1980, St. Vincent's had a maternity home and two infant programs: the Residential Program, which existed from the beginning; and the Shift Care Program (St. Jude Baby Village), which began April 1972. In both, each child's educative program was individually designed for him after he was screened and tested by a professional.

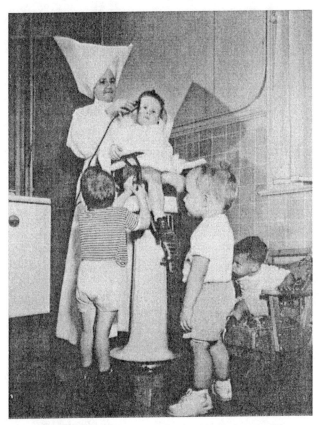

Sister Mary Elizabeth lines children up for haircuts. (Photo by Ray Trahan, courtesy Sally Schreiber)

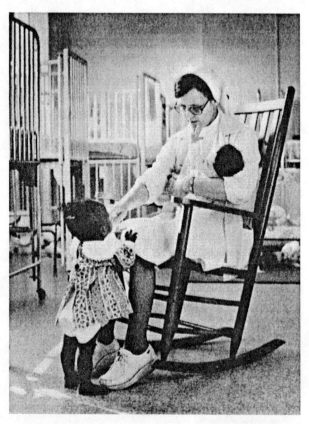

Sister rocks an infant and consoles a toddler (1981).
(Photo by Frank Methe, courtesy Sally Schreiber)

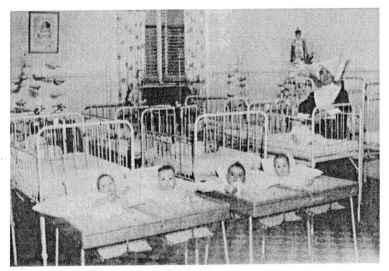

St. Vincent's nursery with babies ages 2-4 months, January 1957.
(Courtesy Sally Schreiber)

Sister Jane Frances rocks an infant at St.
Vincent's. (Photo by Frank Methe,
courtesy Sally Schreiber)

St. Vincent's had a large number of volunteers: high school and college students and mature adults. Volunteers from the League of St. Jude gave their time with the babies in the Shift Care Program.

Also during this time, a major renovation was in progress. Drafty halls, inadequate plumbing, and dangerous balconies made it no place for little children. Most purchasers would raze such a building and rebuild, but Associated Catholic Charities decided to renovate, keeping the exterior as historically accurate as possible. Most of the workmen had to be skilled craftsmen, because nothing was standardized or pre-cut. All the old doors and windows had to be re-worked, and material had to be found that matched the originals.

During the 1980s, Associated Catholic Charities began placing orphans in registered and approved foster homes, where, they felt, they could live in an actual home environment. Associated Catholic Charities still provides funds for childcare to the foster parents.

The upkeep of enormous homes like St. Vincent's and the staff required to care for the home and the children were no longer warranted. In 1988, St. Vincent's program relocated to other places in the city. It still offers an out-patient maternity clinic, pregnancy counseling (ACCESS Pregnancy/Referral Centers), and adoption services.

In 1992, Sally and Peter Schreiber purchased the building and renovated it for a guesthouse, one of their inns under the title Prytania Inns. It was transformed into a European-style guesthouse and furnished in "Victorian New Orleans," according to their brochure, with ceiling fans, wicker furniture, and a large courtyard—all of which evoke the feeling of the antebellum South. St. Vincent's Guest House is listed on the National Register of Historic Places as a contributing element of the Lower Garden District Historic District.

The charity box outside St. Vincent's, 1992. Owner Sally Schreiber found it in pieces and restored it. (Courtesy Sally Schreiber)

St. Vincent Infant Asylum, 1507 Magazine, 1995. Purchased in 1992 by Peter and Sally Schreiber, now a guesthouse under the title Prytania Inns. (Photo by Tracy)

St. Elizabeth's Home

In 1954, St. Elizabeth's Guild was organized to help the teen-age girls and staff. Furnishings for the apartments, laundry equipment, and air conditioning for the living quarters were some of the things the Guild made possible.

In 1955, The Dads' Club grew out of the need to have men involved in the program fulfilling the role of "Dad."

A history of St. Elizabeth's written in 1961, its 125th anniversary, stated that girls living at St. Elizabeth's attended a number of high schools and grade schools in the city and participated in the full curriculum of those schools. They used Public Service buses, paid for by the institution, for transportation to and from school daily. The girls lived dormitory style. Later, dormitories were divided into 2-4 girl bedrooms. The girls were allowed to work in the community, visit friends, and have dates. There were rules and regulations, of course, just as in any good home.

In 1971, there were sixty girls between the ages of six and eighteen still living at St. Elizabeth's. In 1975, St. Vincent Infant & Maternity Home and St. Elizabeth's Home became a part of Associated Catholic Charities of New Orleans, Incorporated.

In 1976, the Daughters of Charity and the Archdiocese of New Orleans entered into a written agreement stating their interest in working jointly and collaboratively to provide and develop social services to meet the needs of the children.

In 1989, St. Elizabeth's merged with the Hope Haven/Madonna Manor complex in Marrero to become the Hope Haven Center, a residential treatment center for boys and girls. Hope Haven Center is also a program of Associated Catholic Charities, Incorporated. The home at 1314 Napoleon was closed, but the program continued.

"There is an evolution of need," said Mary Sutton, administrator of St. Elizabeth's from 1983 to 1989, when

St. Elizabeth's Home in the 1970s. (Photo by Walter Moses, courtesy Daughters of Charity)

Fun time at St. Elizabeth's when the Roman Chewing Candy man came by. (Courtesy Daughters of Charity)

Wedding of a former resident of St. Elizabeth's in the chapel. (Photo by Terry Friedman, courtesy Daughters of Charity)

Children at St. Elizabeth's exclaim over a giant external tank cake donated to the home by Michoud Aerospace. On the left is Barbara Lombard. Mary Sutton, administrator of St. Elizabeth's at the time this photo was taken, is in the center. The woman on the right is Barbara Ory. (Courtesy Daughters of Charity)

Standing in front of the St. Elizabeth's Home are members of the committee for the Beautiful Activists Benefit that was held Sept. 5, 1974, at the New Orleans Fairgrounds. Chairwoman, Mrs. Raymond F. Salmen (right); her vice-chairmen, Mrs. Felix W. Gaudin (left) and Mrs. Thomas Soniat (center); others unidentified. (Photo by Paul Rica, courtesy Daughters of Charity)

the building was closed. "In Margaret Haughery's day, when yellow fever epidemics swept the city, leaving hundreds of children parentless, there was need for these enormous three- and four-story buildings where children could be housed and fed and cared for. Today the needs are different."

Ms. Sutton explained that in the 1980s and 1990s, although St. Elizabeth's Home was still functioning, it was not an orphanage. The children living there were not necessarily parentless. They were there because they could not grow up in their own homes due to some family problem. It might be a financial problem, or it might have to do with drugs, alcohol, or child abuse. These problems have to be adressed with every member of the family. This might be done by private therapists, the counseling department of Associated Catholic Charities, or other agencies such as Family Service of Greater New Orleans.

"The ideal solution," said Ms. Sutton, "is to keep the child in his own home with therapy and training for the family. If this is possible, they are all taught family skills. If it is not possible, the child might be put in therapeutic foster care/family care with adults who have been trained in treatment procedures similar to those in a treatment center."

There is a continuum of care given by Associated Catholic Charities beginning with the child's own home, then possibly foster care. If this is unsuccessful, group home care might be the answer, or placement in a residential facility. Finally, if necessary, there is hospital care, but this is not a service of Associated Catholic Charities.

St. Elizabeth's did not discontinue serving these children in 1989; it *relocated*. Hope Haven Center is now the umbrella title for the residential treatment program. Under that title, Hope Haven and Madonna Manor are for boys; St. Elizabeth is for girls.

Today, specialized treatment by a psychologist or social worker is tailored to the needs of each individual child.

This includes education, psychotherapy, everything that is going on with that child. Referrals are accepted from the Louisiana state foster care and juvenile justice systems.

When it is determined that a child needs to be removed from his own home, he can be placed in an emergency shelter, such as the Methodist Home of New Orleans on the corner of Washington Avenue and Annunciation.

An example of the "evolution of need" to which Ms. Sutton referred is clearly seen in the Jewish Community Center, which was once the site of a Jewish orphanage. The orphanage was torn down and now the JCC offers community services more in keeping with today's needs. When the German Protestant Orphan Asylum closed its program, it sold the property. The proceeds from the sale of the property endowed a foundation known as the German Protestant Orphan Asylum Foundation (GPOA), which continues to fund social services programs.

An organization active in foster care today is Raintree House on Eighth Street in New Orleans. Laura Jensen, director at Raintree, explained that their organization, formerly called The Protestant Home for Babies, used to have a maternity home for unwed mothers and a home for babies. But by the 1970s, unwed mothers began staying at home with their families and there was little need for the maternity house. It was therefore changed to Raintree House, a refuge for young girls abused by their families. A second program, Raintree Family Care, provides foster care for children referred to Raintree by their schools as being at high risk for abuse. A fourth program is the Raintree Case Management Program, which helps families find the resources needed to keep a disabled child at home. The goal of all of these programs is to prevent institutionalization. This is so unlike Margaret's day, when there were no trained specialists in the field, only women with warm hearts and great compassion like Margaret and the Sisters of Charity.

St. Elizabeth's Home, first located in the 2000 block of Magazine Street in 1854, was established here at 1314 Napoleon Avenue in 1871. The architect-builder was Thomas Mulligan. The building was purchased by Stan and Anne Rice in 1993.
(Photo by Tracy)

In 1989, it was decided that St. Elizabeth's building at 1314 Napoleon Avenue, like St. Vincent's building, was too large for the use of Associated Catholic Charities, since much of their work was being done in family homes or group homes. In addition, the enormous building needed total renovation.

By 1993, the St. Elizabeth's building was deteriorating. It was purchased by Anne and Stan Rice from the Daughters of Charity, who had owned the property for 131 years. It has been beautifully renovated and is one of the most recognizable structures in the city. It is listed on the National Register of Historic Places.

The Louise

In 1921, the complex of both buildings facing 1404 Clio Street—the New Orleans Female Orphan Asylum and the Louise Home—was renamed the Louise Home Day Care Center, commonly referred to as "The Louise." It was owned by the Achdiocese of New Orleans.

Young ladies found in "The Louise" a large reception room, a private parlor, laundry service, and two meals a day—all for $5.25 a week if they were willing to share a room. According to a newspaper article from that time, The Louise Home "fulfills the requirements of the most fastidious, and the moderate cost brings within reach . . . comfort and absolute safety so totally absent in the public boarding house."

A scrapbook kept by the Daughters of Charity charts events held annually at the Louise Home: showers for linens and household furnishings, a Depression Party in 1931, a Halloween Party in 1932. In the 1960s there were bridal announcements of former residents and later, pictures of their babies.

In 1966, the old orphanage building was demolished, after being damaged by Hurricane Betsy the previous year.

The New Orleans Female Orphan Asylum building at 1404 Clio Street was used as a home for young working women through the 1950s. During that time, it was called "The Louise." It was demolished in 1966 after Hurricane Betsy damaged it in 1965. The children on the balcony were from the building directly behind it, a day care center, c. 1950. (Courtesy Waldemar S. Nelson)

The Louise Day Nursery Building, a day care center that was built in 1870, was obscured for decades by the former New Orleans Female Orphan Asylum building. (Courtesy Waldemar S. Nelson)

At that time, there were only forty working girls living in the old orphanage. The auxiliary building still housed the nursery. At last, when the old building came down, the second building could be seen facing Clio Street with a large vacant area before it, which, because of the needs of a new century and a new way of life, became a parking lot. But the story was not over yet.

In 1993, Waldemar S. Nelson was looking for just such a parking lot for his employees. When he inquired about the lot with the Archdiocese, he was asked, "Why don't you buy the Louise Day Nursery Building?" In so doing, he would not only save a historic property from the wrecking ball but also contribute to the community in general.

The three-story, red-brick building, vacant since 1976, was slated for demolition after the nursery moved to Louisiana Avenue. Nelson could have used the additional space for parking, but he agreed to buy and renovate the building and allow the church next door to use the parking lot on weekends.

After decades of relative obscurity, the old auxiliary building, now officially called the Louise Day Nursery Building, was purchased by Nelson on April 8, 1993. It has been renovated into an apartment house, without the exterior being altered. A child's painting of a boy and girl shaking hands, restored by Nelson's granddaughter Rebecca Frost, decorates the exterior wall, reminding passersby that children once ran and played here. Like St. Vincent's Guest House, the Louise Day Nursery Building is listed on the National Register of Historic Places as a contributing element of the Lower Garden District Historic District.

Rebecca Frost, granddaughter of Waldemar S. Nelson, at work refurbishing the old painting that adorned the Louise Day Nursery Building. (Courtesy Waldemar S. Nelson)

The interior of the Louise Day Nursery Building, restored as an apartment building, shows the 1870 date of construction. (Photo by Tracy)

The iron fence around Margaret's statue was donated by Waldemar S. Nelson and Company, Incorporated. Celebrating its installation are (left to right) Louise Martin of the Magazine Street Business Association, Waldemar S. Nelson, Florence Schornstein of the Parkway and Park Commission, Brenda Pumphrey of Parkway Partners, Mary Len Costa of the Audubon Institute and of the Margaret Place Restoration Project, Lydia Schmalz of the Coliseum Square Association, and Kenneth H. Nelson of Waldemar S. Nelson and Company, Incorporated. (Courtesy Waldemar S. Nelson)

17

Ladies' Ancient Order of Hibernians, Margaret Haughery Division, Sends Annual "Rose" to Tralee

The Margaret Haughery Club

"I think if Margaret were living today, she would be a woman's liberationist," said Mrs. Louis S. Meridier, chairwoman of Margaret Haughery Day sponsored by the Margaret Haughery Club in 1972. She was being interviewed by a reporter from a local newspaper. On the ninetieth anniversary of Margaret's death, the members of the club placed a wreath at her statue. Doing the honors were Mrs. Meridier, chairwoman of Margaret Haughery Day; Mrs. George Dewhirst, president; and Mrs. Daniel C. Block, financial secretary of the club.

The Margaret Haughery Club was founded in 1948 by Mrs. Hugh Kelley for the purpose of providing the children of some orphan home or institution in or near New Orleans, regardless of race or creed, with toys or gifts that they wanted for Christmas. The club started with only five members, but in less than a year, its membership was forty-eight. At one time, it reached a peak of ninety-two members.

The club's members were all married women without children who provided gifts for impoverished children at Christmas. It was held in high regard by the city of New Orleans. "Pie" Dufour once mentioned it in his column as a living monument to Margaret. The following is an excerpt from an editorial in the *New Orleans States* in 1949:

> Every now and then a group of women organize them-
> selves into a unit that does a real good in the commu-
> nity. Such a group is the new Margaret Haughery Club.
>   In the simple language of its president [and founder]
> Mrs. Hugh Kelley: "We wanted children. God didn't give
> us any children. So we're acting as Santa Claus to 46
> orphans to whom God hasn't given any parents."

Ladies' Ancient Order of Hibernians, Margaret Haughery Division

The Margaret Haughery Club has now died away, but
another organization exists in her honor, the Ladies'
Ancient Order of Hibernians, Margaret Haughery Division.

A men's organization called the Ancient Order of
Hibernians dates back to 1836 (when the religious build-
ings were in danger). It ceased to function after World War
II, but was reactivated in 1989. When the National
Convention of the Ancient Order of Hibernians was to be
held in New Orleans in 1992 at the Hilton, Mrs. Mary Ann
McGrath Swaim was asked to put together a Ladies'
Ancient Order of Hibernians.

"We decided to call our division the Margaret Haughery
Division, not to be confused with the Margaret Haughery
Club of the 1970s," said Mrs. Swaim. "The men's division is
called the Archbishop Hannon Division. We are an international nonprofit organization."

Members of the Margaret Haughery Division are ladies
of Irish descent who are practicing Catholics. A wife of a
man of Irish descent may also belong. In this new organization, it is not a requirement that a woman be childless.

One of the activities of the LAOH Margaret Haughery
Division is to raise money for the missions. Another is the
annual competition for the selection of the Rose of Tralee,
under the direction of Mrs. Nora Lambert.

Three winners of the Rose of Tralee Contest from New Orleans (left to right): Jennifer Coleman (1992), Megan O'Neil (1995), and Kathleen Shea Plasse (1993). Kacee Schexnayder (1994) is not pictured. The annual winner, sponsored by the Ladies' Ancient Order of Hibernians, takes a trip to Ireland to compete for International Rose of Tralee.

Rose of Tralee 1996 Melissa Marie Black.

The Rose of Tralee

In this competition, a young lady of Irish descent from New Orleans is selected from a number of contestants to win a two-week trip to Ireland to compete in the International Rose of Tralee Contest. Nine candidates are sent from North America. A total of thirty-two are sent to Tralee from around the world for a final selection of the year's Rose of Tralee.

The first five Roses sent from New Orleans were Jennifer Coleman (1992), Kathleen Shea Plasse (1993), Kacee Schexnayder (1994), Megan O'Neil (1995), and Melissa Marie Black (1996).

The selection is made on the basis of poise and personality. The judges meet with the young ladies at several social functions to be able to assess these qualities in the candidates. Later, they ask the candidates several questions about their heritage, their families, their ambitions, and their reasons for wanting to go to Ireland. At an appointed time, in closed conference, the judges take a ballot and select a winner.

What a wonderful tribute to Margaret Gaffney Haughery, who came to us from Ireland, that we should send an Irish lass back to Margaret's native land as an emissary from her chosen country! It makes her life and her magnificent efforts come full circle.

18

A Venerated Monument

By 1978, A LARGE CRACK HAD APPEARED in the pedestal of Margaret's statue and a finger on her right hand was missing. The surface of the statue was deteriorating due to years of exposure to the weather.

New Orleans sculptress Angela Gregory spearheaded a campaign to save the statue, bringing its condition to the attention of Phyllis Parun, the visual arts coordinator of the Art Information Bureau of the city library. The two then spoke to members of the Historic District Landmarks Commission. After that, Parun; Saundra Levy, director of the Historic District Landmarks Commission; Geoffrey Platt, director of the Arts Council of Greater New Orleans; and Rany Gregson, deputy director of the city's Office of Property Management, met to discuss the future of Margaret's statue.

One of the problems in saving the monument was determining who owned it. No city agency claimed responsibility. An ordinance had been passed in 1925 creating a board to oversee the statue, but there was no record of what happened after that. Parun also contacted stone experts for advice about what should be done.

In 1988, the statue of Margaret got a good cleaning and a bit of repair work. To rejuvenate the statue, the project committee enlisted the services of Frank G. Matero, director of Columbia University's Center for Historic

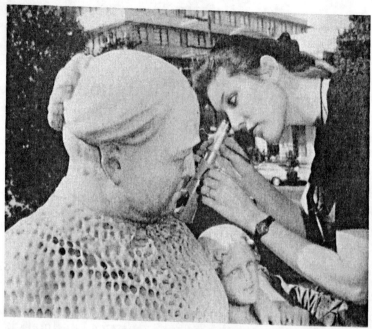

Phyllis Tudor takes scrapings of Margaret Haughery's shawl to plan a solution for cleaning and restoration. (Staff photo by Bryan Berteaux, November 1988, courtesy The Times-Picayune Publishing Company)

Preservation. He came to New Orleans with his assistant, Phyllis Tudor, a Columbia University graduate student who was doing her thesis on marble cleaning and consolidation. The initial visit was to determine the type of marble that was used and to make a damage assessment. They studied their findings in New York and then worked out the proper procedures for refurbishing the statue.

Matero explained that a condition called "sugaring" develops with time, largely attributable to acid rain. "Sugaring" results in loss of detail and the surface of the statue becomes dull. "The New Orleans climate," he said, "encourages biological growth, such as a darkening mossy growth that seeps into crevices." (The detailing in Margaret's shawl is an obvious prey to such growth.)

Because the statue is located so close to the river, the deterioration was accelerated by pollutants coming from the nearby Mississippi River Bridge traffic. Scrapings were analyzed, and the proper solutions for cleaning were prepared and used.

"It is impossible to make a statue look new," said Matero, "nor would we want to see that done. We can't reverse time. What is important is that Margaret stays outdoors, here in her own environment."

Margaret's statue located in the maze of the Camp Street upramp and Camp and Prytania streets, February 1973. (Photo by Pat Patterson, courtesy The Times-Picayune Publishing Company)

The Camp Street upramp to the Mississippi River Bridge under demolition, September 1994. Photo shows how close the ramp was to St. Theresa's Church, the Louise Day Nursery Building beyond, and the Margaret statue beyond that. (Staff photo by Matt Rose, courtesy The Times-Picayune Publishing Company)

19

Down with the Upramp, the "Berlin Wall" of the Lower Garden District

TIMES CHANGE AND THE NEEDS of a city change. Above all else, New Orleans needed a bridge across the Mississippi River to Algiers and Gretna that could be approached from the Central Business District. The bridge was completed in 1958 and so were the upramps. These lengthy approaches to the bridge affected many parts of the city, changing their beauty and personality.

There was little outcry when the state transportation planners and the Mississippi River Bridge Authority built the ramp on Camp Street in the late 1950s. At that time, the neighborhood preservation movement was in its infancy and carried little influence in the Lower Garden District. No one dreamed that the trickle of West Bank-bound traffic would grow to 10,000 vehicles a day.

The Camp Street upramp, curving toward the river from Melpomene, turned a neighborhood rich in nineteenth-century architecture and history into a speedway for West Bank commuters. In existence for thirty-six years, it edged right up to and almost wrapped around Margaret's statue. There, where traffic converged, the statue stood in a barrage of noise and fumes and traffic jams, as hundreds of drivers rushed to work alongside Margaret Park.

No longer was the statue visible for anything but a quick glance as one approached the bridge. It was no longer in a setting where it could be admired for its artistic and historic value.

Neighborhood pressure for the ramp's removal began in the 1970s, soon after the establishment of the Coliseum Square Association. In 1977, fearing that neighborhood leaders would use the area's designation as a national historic district to halt the bridge work, state officials agreed in writing to tear down the ramp.

But no date was set for the demolition. Target dates came and went, but the ramp remained. Word finally came from the Secretary of the State Department of Transportation and Development. A test-case closing had shown that eliminating the ramp would not impede the flow of traffic to the bridge. This came after fifteen years of deferred promises that were based on the 1977 Memorandum of Agreement formulated by the National Advisory Council on Historic Preservation, an agreement signed by the U.S. Coast Guard, the Louisiana State Historic Preservation Office, the Louisiana Department of Transportation and Development, and the Mississippi River Bridge Authority.

Finally, in 1993-94, heavy machinery moved in, massive chunks of concrete were broken, and the ramp came down. After all signs are removed that a ramp once disfigured this historic neighborhood, a wide roadway, double-laned on each side, will be built over the Coliseum/Camp streets, which come to a joining point in the block that fronts St. Theresa of Avila Church. Then a landscaped neutral ground with a little park will be developed in the center.

The ramp's removal was due largely to the efforts of the Coliseum Square Association and to individuals like Lydia and Howard Schmalz, recipients of the Harnett T. Kane Preservation Award for 1995. As president of the association in 1993-94, Mrs. Schmalz put forth outstanding efforts that led to the final removal of the Camp Street upramp.

Commuters have now been routed to other approaches

Margaret sits atop her pedestal as a crane and heavy machinery mop up after the removal of the Camp Street upramp. (Photo by Tracy)

The Louise Day Nursery Building and St. Theresa's Church behind it are hemmed in by heavy machinery removing concrete chunks, the remains of the Camp Street upramp, 1995. (Photo by Tracy)

and people in the Lower Garden District are celebrating. "It should never have been there," said Camille Strachan, a lawyer who began work for the ramp's removal in the early 1970s. "All I want to do is celebrate."

On October 2, 1994, the Coliseum Square Association threw a celebration party that featured traditional jazz music and champagne. Everyone was invited. The Camp Street upramp, the "Berlin Wall" between Coliseum Square and the Lafayette Square and Warehouse districts, was coming down at last!

Already, houses on Coliseum Street are being renovated in anticipation of the newly developed neighborhood, which will be a showplace for the city. Now, once again, Margaret's statue will have suitable landscaping and the proper backdrop for the memory of a woman who was one of a kind, a woman whose life was dedicated to the poor and the orphaned children of the city of New Orleans.

The Klotz Cracker Factory, run by Bernard Klotz, Margaret's foster son, shipped tins of crackers, cookies, and candies nationwide and worldwide in 5-, 10-, 15-, 20-, and 25-pound tins like this one. (Courtesy Sheila Larmann)

Epilogue: Thoughts on Margaret

Father Lelièvre, a priest of the Congregation from France, who came to New Orleans in 1868 to help organize the establishment of the Little Sisters of the Poor, wrote of Margaret in 1880:

> At first sight you would never guess it was the Irish Margaret. When you arrive at the entry of this immense building, four stories high, with the single word MARGARET sculpted on the front in large letters, you say to yourself, "This building must have cost at least $150,000." You enter. On the threshold, a short, stout woman appears. She is neither young nor pretty, wearing a cotton dress and a cap, with both hands in the pockets of her linsey-woolsey apron.
> "I would like to speak with Mrs. Margaret."
> "I am Margaret, sir."

And so she was—the head of a baking business with two hundred workmen baking and distributing millions of dollars worth of bread, cake, and biscuits each year, with thirty wagons transporting the goods into town and to the shiploading docks. But she is also the MARGARET who is at the head of every charitable subscription list, who supports two hundred children of an orphanage and who now provides food for half the old people of the Little Sisters of the Poor. I consider her the best and most astonishing of bakers who has put a hand in dough since the days of Pharoah!

Author's Note

While this book was in production, I received a letter from Michael O'Rourke, great-great-grandnephew of Margaret Gaffney Haughery on her mother's side. He had read my June 11, 1995, article "Still a Pillar of the Community" about Margaret in the *Times-Picayune*. He was happy that a book was being written about his illustrious ancestor.

His letter offered a brief summary of facts about Margaret's life, confirming much of my research. He confirmed that Margaret's mother, Margaret O'Rourke, was a descendant of the O'Rourke tribe who were titled "Sovereign Prince of Breffni, County Leitrim."

Margaret was born in Carrigallen, County Leitrim, and her people still live there, according to Michael O'Rourke. Her older brother Thomas, who remained behind in Ireland when Margaret and her parents emigrated, married Catherine Healy of Aldlogher in 1839. They had a daughter, Mary, in 1843. Thomas and his family later emigrated to Baltimore, where their descendants were still living as late as the 1950s and where they may still be living. Margaret's sister Mary, who stayed behind in Ireland, lived all of her life in Tully.

Margaret often spoke of Killeshandra, County Cavan, and many who have written about her called this her birthplace. While it is true that she visited Killeshandra often, since the Leitrim/Cavan boundary line was so close to her home, she and all of the O'Rourkes were from County Leitrim.

When Margaret emigrated, she would have spoken only Gaelic, according to Mr. O'Rourke, and would have had to learn English in America. When Margaret signed her will, she could not write, for she signed her will with an *X*, but she taught herself to read a little.

MARY LOU WIDMER

Bibliography

Books

Baudier, Roger. *The Catholic Church in Louisiana.* New Orleans: n.p., 1939.

Christovich, Mary Louise, Roulhac Toledano, Betsy Swanson, and Pat Holden. *New Orleans Architecture, Volume II: The American Sector.* Gretna, La.: Pelican, 1972.

Huber, Leonard V. *New Orleans: A Pictorial History.* Gretna, La.: Pelican, 1991.

Huber, Leonard V., Peggy McDowell, and Mary Louise Christovich. *New Orleans Architecture, Volume III: The Cemeteries.* Edited by Samuel Wilson, Jr. Gretna, La.: Pelican, 1974.

King, Grace. *The Place and the People.* New York: n.p., 1899.

Martinez, Raymond J. *The Immortal Margaret Haughery.* New Orleans: Industries Publishing Agency, n.d.

Murphy, Edward F. *Angel of the Delta.* Garden City, N.Y.: Hanover House, 1958.

Federal Writers' Project of the Works Progress Administration. *New Orleans City Guide.* Boston: Houghton Mifflin Co., 1938.

Strousse, Flora. *Margaret, Breadwoman of New Orleans.* New York: P. J. Kennedy & Sons, n.d.

Wilson, Samuel, Jr., and Bernard Lemann. *New Orleans Architecture, Volume I: The Lower Garden District.* Gretna, La.: Pelican, 1971.

Articles

Baudier, Roger. "Margaret Haughery, Laundress, Dairy Maid, Baker, Philantropist, and 'friend of orphans' to be honored by Southern Bakers." *The Mixer,* May 1929.

Collier, Alberta. "Oil Portrait of Margaret Haughery in Presbytere Exhibit Seems Right." *The Times-Picayune,* 19 December 1971.

"Did You Know?" *Rider's Digest.* N.O. Public Service, 8 January 1973.

"Her Loaves for Charity." *New Orleans States,* 1929.

Houston, David. "Story of One of the Greatest New Orleans Benefactors Related." *The Times-Picayune New Orleans States,* 9 February 1958.

King, Grace. "Margaret." *Harper's Bazaar,* 15 October 1887.

"Splendid Group of Asylums." *Louisiana Scrapbook #2,* n.p.

Lynch, Elizabeth. "Margaret Gaffney Haughery." *The Journal of the American Irish Historic Society.* Vol. 28, 1929-30.

"Margaret Gaffney Haughery." *Morning Star* and *Catholic Messenger,* 13 July 1884.

McGrath, Adrian N. "Remembering Margaret Haughery." *Irish Eyes.* Phoenix: Masterpiece Publishing, Inc., September 1994.

"Orphan's Friend." *The Times-Picayune,* 8 October 1981.

Pitts, Stella. "Margaret Spent Her Life Helping Orphans and the Poor." *The Times-Picayune,* 25 April 1976.

Ponchartrain, Blake. "New Orleans Know-It-All." *Gambit,* 3 March 1992.

Thomann, Emily Wengard. "Margaret of New Orleans." *The Catholic World* 143 (no. 853), April 1936.

Thomas, Lanny. "Margaret." *States-Item,* 8 March 1978.

Interviews

Jensen, Laura, director of Raintree House. Telephone interview with author. June 28, 1996.

Nelson, Waldemar S., purchaser of The Louise building. Interview with author. May 17, 1995.

Schreiber, Sally, purchaser of St. Vincent Orphan Asylum building. Interview with author. April 24, 1995.

Sister Mary Hermenia Muldrey, R.S.M., author of *Abounding in Mercy,* the story of Mother Austin Carroll. Authority on Margaret Haughery. Interview with author. April 22, 1995.

Sutton, Mary, administrator of St. Elizabeth's 1983-89.

Interview with author. "The Evolution of Need." July 15, 1995.

Swaim, Mary Ann McGrath, president of Ladies' Order of Ancient Hibernians, Margaret Haughery Division. Telephone interview with author. May 21, 1995.

Index

Printed in the United Kingdom
by Lightning Source UK Ltd.
100494UKS00001B/34